Cross-examined

Cross-examined

The life-changing power
of the death of Jesus

MARK MEYNELL

Inter-Varsity Press

INTER-VARSITY PRESS
38 De Montfort Street, Leicester LE1 7GP, England
Email: ivp@ivp-editorial.co.uk
Website: www.ivpbooks.com

First published 2001
Reprinted 2001, 2003, 2004
Second edition (with study guide) 2005

British Library Cataloguing in Publication Data
A catalogue record for this book is available from the British Library.

ISBN–13: 978–1–84474–101–4
ISBN–10: 1–84474–101–X

Set in Dante 10.5/13pt
Typeset in Great Britain by CRB Associates, Reepham, Norfolk
Printed in Great Britain by CPD (Wales), Ebbw Vale

Inter-Varsity Press is the publishing division of the Universities and Colleges Christian Fellowship (formerly the Inter-Varsity Fellowship), a student movement linking Christian Unions in universities and colleges throughout Great Britain, and a member movement of the International Fellowship of Evangelical Students. For more information about local and national activities write to UCCF, 38 De Montfort Street, Leicester LE1 7GP, email us at email@uccf.org.uk, or visit the UCCF website at www.uccf.org.uk.

Contents

To Rachel
who was
excited by,
endured and
encouraged
this book

Preface

It has not been straightforward converting a preacher into a writer! If this has been successful, it is due to the efforts of a large number of friends who have helped at various stages of writing. While many deserve thanks, there is only space to mention those who have read parts of the various drafts: Chris Barton, Jez Carr, Don Carson, Simon Gathercole, Nancy Heeb, Paul Houghton, Jem Hovil, David Jackman, Anna May, Ed Moll, Andrew Nicholls, Terry Pratt, Mike Reeder, Helen Shawyer, Matt Sherratt, Helen Terry, Steve Timmis and Garry Williams. Thanks are due to my two prayer partners, Matt Porter and Alex Absalom, whose encouragement and prayers have been invaluable. I am especially grateful to my colleagues Hugh Palmer and Tim Davies who, as well as being prepared to keep reading chapters, spared me some of the burdens of a busy ministry at Christ Church to give me writing-time.

Suggestions about different parts of the book offered by various audiences (of students and others at Fulwood and at Spring Harvest Word Alive) have been very helpful. In particular, Philip Duce, Theological Books Editor at IVP, has given vital support and assistance. Where there are errors of judgment or interpretation, however, the blame lies squarely with me.

Finally, my greatest gratitude goes to Rachel, my wife. The sacrifices she made so that I could work on this book on and off for nearly two years have been the single most important factor in its completion. She very patiently encouraged me throughout, so it is only right that I dedicate this book to her.

Mark Meynell
Christ Church, Fulwood, Sheffield
December 2000
To the Greater Glory of God

Preface to Study Guide edition

Some friends have questioned the wisdom in not printing out the Bible passages at the top of each chapter in full. This was actually deliberate (quite apart from space-saving). The aim was to encourage readers to read with their Bibles open and thus get a sense of these passages *in situ*. It was hoped that this would encourage a reading process that is perhaps more active than passive, and thus more engaged. A forlorn hope, perhaps! Nevertheless, please do try to read through the particular passage in the Bible *before* reading the relevant chapter here.

A handful of people have contributed to the process of making minor revisions and devising the new Study Guide: Garry Williams, Nick and Cecilia Hiscocks and, here at KEST, Jennie Martone and our two 2004–2005 interns, Adam Johnson and David Kim. I am immensely grateful to them for their help.

Mark Meynell
Kampala Evangelical School of Theology (KEST), Uganda
April 2005

Part 1. Cross-examined
1. In the dock

Please read John 18

God on trial

Time slows down in the middle of the night. When you cannot get to sleep, the ticks of the alarm clock seem to get louder, and the minutes feel like hours. The more you long for sleep, the more awake you feel and, whether you like it or not, you have extra thinking-time on your hands. Those fears, regrets and doubts, which remain at the back of the mind during the day, come to the fore in the restlessness of an unsettled night. Perhaps it was an unkind word here, or a missed opportunity there. Perhaps it is the dread of an imminent exam, or the real sense of regret at a failed relationship.

Doubts and fears can then quickly give way to big questions. Perhaps the most common are 'Why?' or 'How could you?' They are vital questions, but awkward. They can apply both to deeply personal situations and to issues that affect the whole world; and it is very often God who ends up being the defendant in our imaginary courtroom. Charges range from the private ('If he is there, why does he seem so remote? He never answered *my* prayers when I needed him most. He never looks after me!') to the global ('How can a world tormented by pain, injustice and evil be compatible with belief in the God of the Bible? Isn't he meant to be powerful and good? So how could he permit nationwide ethnic cleansing? How can he claim to be powerful *and* good?') The singer Robbie Williams found himself confronted by these sorts of questions on his trip to flood-ravaged Mozambique as a UNICEF ambassador. In a subsequent interview, he said, 'You come here and you say, "Where's their God, where's their God, why? Why has that happened? Why were they born here, why do they have a flood and why do they have another flood?"' [1]

Even if you are a convinced Christian, you cannot deny that these questions are formidable. Being a Christian does not provide immunity from such doubts, and glib answers to those questions will never do. Irving Greenberg, a writer on the Holocaust, commented on the issue of the existence of God in a suffering world in these shocking terms: 'No statement, theological or otherwise, should be made that would not be credible in the presence of burning children.' [2] That is a horrific thought, yet is one which tragedies like the Holocaust will not let us dismiss. After the uniquely bloody twentieth century, the charges against God seem impregnable. Is there *anything* credible that can be said? Is it any wonder that the century that has witnessed more suffering than any other has also seen the most hostility to belief in a good, creator God? Whether people spend their nights wrestling with the problem or not, many construct their own challenge to such a God. If he is there, they want answers.

There are biblical precedents for this, of course. The writer of the Psalms could be ruthlessly honest about the doubts and questions he wanted God to address (read, for example, Psalms 22, 55 and 142). He endured many a sleepless night. Then there was Job, who suffered such intolerable hardship that he experienced a major crisis of faith (read, for example, Job 23 – 24). Nevertheless, despite their doubts, both Job and the psalmist managed to persist in their trust in God. Job, for one, even received a revitalizing vision, described at the end of the book (Job 38 – 42). It did not provide him with easy answers, nor leave him unchallenged, but it did vindicate his persistent trust in God. Job was convinced that although many of his questions remain unresolved, God was *still* good.

These precedents indicate that questioning God may not in itself be wrong. They also indicate that trusting God despite terrible circumstances is not impossible. How this might be we will go on to explore. However, before we proceed, we must be conscious of our motives when we bring our questions to God, because they may not be as innocent as we might think. C. S. Lewis deliberately confronts us with the step we are taking:

> The ancient man approached God (or even the gods) as the accused person approaches his judge. For the modern man the roles are reversed. He is the judge: God is in the dock. He is quite a kindly judge: if God should have a reasonable defence for being the god who permits war, poverty and disease, he is ready to listen to it. The trial may even end in God's acquittal. But the important thing is that man is on the bench and God in the dock.[3]

That is a significant development, and one which at the very least should cause us to proceed with caution.

A king on trial

Lewis describes a relatively modern phenomenon, but the New Testament does contain an ancient 'divine trial'. Like so many of our imaginary trials, this one happened in the middle of the night nearly 2,000 years ago. This was no figment of a fevered imagination, however. It occurred on a very cold night, such that those who were awake struggled to keep warm by huddling around dying fires. The air was heavy with betrayal and conspiracy. An essential difference between Job's story and this one lies in the fact that very few, if any, of those who conducted the trial realized the true identity of the defendant. He claimed to be King of the Jews, but his interrogators gave very little credence, if any, to the possibility that this might actually be true. They were unwaveringly hostile and determined to eliminate him. Summary execution would have been preferable, but was impossible; as citizens of a subject nation, the Jewish leaders were forced to resort to conspiring with the Roman authorities to achieve their ends.

Jesus of Nazareth was on trial for his life. He had been adored and vilified in almost equal measure. Surely, if he really had been God's king, trial and execution at the hands of human beings would be inconceivable, wouldn't it? What a ridiculous idea! That in itself merely confirmed the Jewish leaders' conviction that he was not who he claimed to be. The great kings of Israel had, of course, been through some difficult situations over the centuries, but none of them had ever endured the ignominy of impeachment proceedings. Jesus couldn't possibly be who he claimed to be; so they no doubt felt safe. Not only that; they felt it was their religious duty to do away with this peasant rabblerouser and ludicrous royal pretender.

During that eventful night, however, something extraordinary happened. All four Gospel-writers describe it, but perhaps none more vividly than John. In John 18, we travel from Jesus' arrest in the garden of Gethsemane to his various trials before the Jewish and Roman authorities. Interlaced is the story of Peter's denials of Jesus, which added to the sense of Jesus' isolation. Be alert to what is happening throughout the account. While the action quickly shifts from the high priest's house to the Roman governor's palace, the constant question behind John's account of the trials is, 'Who is really in control here?'

First is Annas (John 18:12–14). He had been the high priest until the Roman authorities deposed him, but he still wielded significant influence in Jerusalem. Several members of his family had actually succeeded him. Intriguingly, John here seems more interested in Annas's son-in-law, Caiaphas, who was the current incumbent as high priest. He writes, 'Caiaphas was the one who had advised the Jews that it would be good if one man died for the people' (John 18:14). That detail is not given merely for identification purposes, since there could be little doubt as to who was in mind. Instead, John mentions it specifically to recall Caiaphas's remark in the Jewish council, the Sanhedrin.[4] Dripping with unconscious irony, Caiaphas had then appealed to Jewish political expediency. His gist was that it would be far better to get rid of just one troublemaker than to give the Romans further grounds for destroying the whole Jewish way of life. Jesus should die for the sake of the nation. Caiaphas, of course, had no idea how close he was to the truth. John saw it, and he wants his readers to see it. Jesus was indeed to die for a purpose – but it was to be for the eternal benefit of all people. Without the slightest appreciation of that fact, Caiaphas was absolutely right. As we shall come to understand, someone as well versed in the Jewish Scriptures as the high priest should have anticipated Jesus' mission.

After Peter's first denial, Jesus' first interrogation got under way (John 18:19–24). The previous verses inform us that it was night. That in itself casts doubt on the legitimacy of the proceedings of Jesus' trial. They were technically illegal if not held during the day,[5] but that was not the only irregularity. It is probable that in contemporary Jewish law it was also illegal to put questions to a defendant at all, since the 'case had to rest on the weight of the testimony of witnesses'.[6] Because control over the proceedings lay in the hands of his opponents, the deck was hopelessly stacked against Jesus. He was a mere carpenter without a legal qualification to his name, and Caiaphas and the Sanhedrin knew what they were doing. What chance did Jesus have against those who could simply rewrite the rules? Nevertheless, Jesus was composed, a fact that forces us to keep asking, 'Who is really in control here?'

In reply to the first questions Jesus had nothing to hide about his activities. Notice how he came back at his accusers: 'Why question me? Ask those who heard me. Surely they know what I said' (John 18:21). Not only was Jesus secure in his innocence, but he also had the confidence to challenge his accusers directly. If we are correct in thinking that it really was illegal to question defendants in Jesus' time, then it should have been members of his audience answering the charges, not Jesus. He had a point. No wonder this challenge brought Jesus a violent blow to the face. Again he was not deterred: 'If I said something wrong . . . testify as to what is wrong. But if I spoke the truth, why did you strike me?' (John 18:23). Jesus was calm and level-headed. He was the one dominating the scene, not Caiaphas.

Before we can fully understand what actually occurred that night, however, we need to move on to Jesus' encounter with the Roman governor, Pontius Pilate. Pilate had an unenviable task. Violence and cruelty were second nature to him, but that did not prevent him feeling torn when confronted by Jesus. He was clearly suspicious of the charges brought against him, so he put the crucial question directly to the defendant: 'Are you the king of the Jews?' (John 18:33). Yet again, Jesus replied with a question: 'Is that your own idea . . . or did others talk to you about me?' (John 18:34). Pilate was indignant and impatient: 'Am I a Jew?' (John 18:35). From his point of view, Jesus was a parochial Jewish problem. It hardly concerned him. Jesus was not Pilate's king. That really would be a preposterous idea . . .

Jesus explained that his kingship was of a different order. He was no revolutionary Che Guevara, no imperialistic Alexander the Great, no tyrannical Caesar. This king sits on an eternal and divine throne. His authority far exceeds that of any human monarch: 'My kingdom is not of this world. If it were, my servants would fight to prevent my arrest by the Jews. But now my kingdom is from another place' (John 18:36). Pilate grasped very little of what Jesus was talking about. He was simply fishing for a clear-cut admission of a claim to the Jewish throne – that would at least give some grounds for accepting the charges against Jesus. Pilate did eventually get what he was after, but it was not in quite the straightforward way he would have wanted: 'You are right in saying I am a king. In fact, for this reason I was born, and for this I came into the world, to testify to the truth. Everyone on the side of truth listens to me' (John 18:37).

Do you notice the tremendous challenge to Pilate there? It is as if Jesus was replying to Pilate's subconscious thoughts: 'Yes, I am your king. If you were on the side of truth, you would accept that.' Implicitly, Jesus was throwing down the gauntlet: 'Are you on the side of truth?' The man in the dock has issued an invitation to his prosecutor. It is an invitation to be aligned with the truth, and so to become subject to this other-worldly king. Superficially, it seems a forlorn and hollow boast, coming as it did from a man on death row with nothing to lose. Jesus here seemed easy to dismiss, and a dismissal was what he received. 'What is truth?' was Pilate's impatient retort (John 18:38).

Was Pilate merely trying to avoid an answer? Or did he genuinely struggle with the existence of objective truth? We shall never know; the conversation ends abruptly with that momentous question. Pilate walked out to give the Jewish leaders his preliminary thoughts. He was initially unable to justify the death penalty, and yet he could see no political alternative to the unjust demands of the Sanhedrin. His struggle between conscience and expediency gave him a restless night of his own. The one who had seemed easy to dismiss was in fact far too compelling. Nevertheless, the fact that his struggle did not stop him executing an innocent man demonstrates that he was not on the side of what he knew to be true. The Roman governor with power over life and death was humiliated by the God-sent king who reveals what is true. Pilate left the gauntlet where it fell.

Prosecution or defence?

Jesus' trials have mystified and provoked readers for centuries. We witness a man at the height of his powers and in full control of himself. Not only that; he seemed in full control of the predicament he was in. Despite this, Jesus made no effort to protect himself. He even restrained his uncomprehending disciples. To top it all, the defence he gave at his trial was nothing if not highly provocative. No right-minded barrister would ever recommend that tactic. To prosecute the judge when he should have been pleading for his life was sheer lunacy! He should have settled for answering the questions, rather than firing them back. It gives the impression that his deliberate plan was to die on the cross . . .

What appears to have been folly was no such thing, however. Jesus' trial actually demonstrates a vital reality. When we put God in the dock, however justified the charges against him might seem, we quickly find that we have searching questions to answer for ourselves. Both Job and Pilate discovered that fact in their different ways, but only one was on the side of truth; only one accepted God's right to do this. Now, technically, a cross-examination in a court of law occurs when a defendant or witness is questioned by an opposing barrister about statements already made. It is a necessary process to verify the soundness of their testimony. However, when God is placed in the dock, there is a cross-examination with a difference. I, the prosecutor, find the tables turned as I seek to challenge God's defence. God, the defendant, has questions to put to me.

We shall discover the same unsettling phenomenon as we explore what happened at the cross. As far as the Bible is concerned, that event is the supreme achievement of God's activity in the world. It was always part of his plan to send Jesus to die there, and Jesus himself deliberately set out on the road to the cross. Astonishingly, it is only through examining the cross that credible answers to so many of the accusations hurled at God can be found. It acts as God's final statement of defence to a suffering world. The one we seek to prosecute answers the charges against himself perfectly. He has nothing to hide. However, as we examine his 'defence', we ourselves are forced on to the defensive. God the accused issues his own challenge. He performs an acutely personal cross-examination of each of us: 'Whose side are *you* on? Are *you* ready to accept the verdict of the truth? Will *you* submit to the king who reveals that truth?' This means that grappling with the cross will never be a light matter, even if that is something we have done many times before. It will always be challenging. So if that is a challenge you are prepared to face, then read on!

Summary

- When we consider the sufferings and injustices of our world, God is very often the one from whom we demand answers.
- While many of these questions are entirely justified, however, we cannot escape our own answerability to God.
- As we shall see, the cross of Jesus is where we are faced with both of these issues: there we find both God's answer to a suffering world and our own answerability to God.

2. 'You can't believe that, can you?'

Please read 1 Corinthians 1:18–25

A symbol that invites ridicule

For many, belief in the God of the Bible seems wishful thinking at best, an obscenity at worst. On more than one occasion, people have said to me, 'You can't honestly expect me to believe all that stuff, can you?' Combine that understandable incredulity with the central premise of Christianity, namely, that the one we worship was executed on a cross, and it all seems absurd. Our over-familiarity with the universal Christian symbol of the cross blinds us to its horror. As comedian Bill Hicks once pointed out with reference to President John F. Kennedy's assassination from a Dallas book depository, 'People who think JFK was a hero don't wear a shotgun on their lapel.'[1]

Consider it once more. On the cross Jesus died. He is the one in whom the hope of every Christian is invested. He is the one who apparently has equality with God, who apparently reveals what God is like, who apparently enables us to know God. Yet he died! On a cross! That wraps up those claims once and for all, surely?

'You can't honestly expect me to believe that, can you?' God's anticipated robust defence to humanity's prosecution never seemed to get off the ground. 'If that's all he can come up with, then there's no point giving him another moment's thought.'

P. D. James is a writer renowned for her intricate and thought-provoking detective novels, but one book has a very different theme. *The Children of Men* describes the world twenty-one years after it has suffered a global pandemic of human infertility. No children have been born anywhere on the planet, and the human race is simply awaiting extinction. England, in common with many other parts of the world, is living under the shadow of dictatorship, but that does not seem to matter to most people. The only important thing for them is dulling their agony through a full immersion in pleasure. Consequently, the book is a parable for our self-indulgent world, and there are many unnerving parallels with our own culture. One of the most striking observations is what happens to religious belief. The narrator describes the renowned preacher of a recently devised religion, one Rosie McClure: 'Rosie ... has virtually abolished the Second Person of the Trinity together with His cross, substituting a golden orb of the sun in glory, like a garish Victorian pub sign. The change was immediately popular. Even to unbelievers like myself, the cross, the stigma of the barbarism of officialdom and of man's ineluctable cruelty, has never been a comfortable symbol.'[2]

The narrator pinpoints the problem precisely. No marketing executive would ever choose the cross for a new corporate logo. How can an ancient instrument of institutional torture and execution possibly be God's answer to a suffering world? What good could it possibly achieve? It is ridiculous. More than that, it is obscene.

Where, then, do we begin in our response to these reasonable and valid questions?

A death that demands interpretation

In apartheid South Africa, township vigilantes used to reserve their most horrific punishment for those they regarded as traitors.

Their kangaroo courts aimed both to execute culprits and to terrify potential traitors. 'Rubber necklace' executions involved the victim being draped with a petrol-filled rubber tyre and then set alight. Apart from the obvious horror that evokes, such a tortured death carried a terrible stigma – the intention was to cause the victim's family and friends maximum shame and humiliation. Crucifixion had similar connotations in the Roman Empire. It was considered so terrible that it was reserved for foreign criminals. A Roman criminal could expect a less agonizing death. The only difference from 'rubber necklacing' lay in its real barbarism. The process of death could last for hours, even days. It deliberately guaranteed a chilling combination of emotional turmoil and physical agony.

Picture yourself as a bystander in Jerusalem on that dark day. Despite the prevalence of crucifixion in the Roman world, Jesus' death would have been particularly poignant. No-one in the city could possibly have been ignorant of the sorts of things people were saying about him. They would have been gossiping about his claims to divinity in all the city's guesthouses and taverns, which would have been overflowing because of the Jewish Passover festivities. Seeing him hanging on that cross must have made those claims seem hollow and pathetic. Furthermore, any good Jew would have known from the Scriptures that such a death could mean only one thing. He must have been abandoned by God. The Old Testament law stated categorically, 'anyone who is hung on a tree is under God's curse' (Deuteronomy 21:23).[3] That surely meant that there was no way his claims could be true. How could he be God and yet at the same time be abandoned by God? It was absurd.

So, as you look up at that tortured and humiliated figure, only one interpretation seems to fit: failure. Jesus obviously had potential. He may even at times have demonstrated great leadership, sublime teaching, and captivating integrity; but his death surely proved his fundamental claims to be wrong. Standing there with the remaining handful of spectators, you perhaps echo the thoughts of those two distraught followers of Jesus as they left Jerusalem for Emmaus two days later: 'we had hoped that he was the one who was going to redeem Israel' (Luke 24:21). The implication, as they uttered these words to their unrecognized fellow-traveller, was that *he was not* going to do so. Failure. As Tim Rice's lyrics for *Jesus Christ, Superstar* had it, Jesus was a 'faded, jaded mandarin'. If any visited the hill called Golgotha in the vain hope of discovering any last-minute grounds for optimism, crushing disappointment was all that awaited them. What people witnessed that day left them in no doubt whatsoever. It was all over. If the cross symbolized anything at all, it was defeat.

Even a defeat as overwhelming as this one can be deceptive, however. Perhaps our culture, more than any other, needs to learn the deceptiveness of appearances. We are so familiar with images and sounds being constantly thrown at us to sell us products we do not really need, or to convince us that someone is genuinely trustworthy and worth electing. Yet, somehow, there seems little awareness of the need to be wary these days. It seems so much easier to accept the face value, rather than to ask too many awkward questions. If people give the death of Jesus a moment's thought (and many do not), they will accept the explanation that first comes to mind. After all, failure does seem the most logical description. Nevertheless, that does not make it an accurate description.

The first Christians were fully convinced of the need to keep the cross central to their beliefs, come what may. The ridicule and incomprehension of their society did not cause them to waver. Why? Because they held to a radically different interpretation, which both the Old Testament and Jesus himself anticipated. What in many ways seemed a genuine defeat (for there is little point trying to deny that execution is defeat) was *also* an astounding victory. More than that, they were convinced that Jesus' victory could only have come about *through* this apparent defeat of the cross. That is what initially makes it so hard to fathom or explain. None of the first Christians felt the difficulties of explaining this more keenly than the apostle Paul, as he sought to bring the news about Jesus Christ to Jews and non-Jews alike. Paul was a unique figure in the first decades of the church, full of both a passionate concern for individuals and a penetrating grasp of Christian truth. His effect on the church was probably more profound than that of any other follower of Jesus.

Paul's first letter to the Christians in Corinth is one of his earliest to be preserved in the Bible. The church there had many problems that urgently required his attention. Apart from anything else, the lifestyle of these young Christians hardly differed from that of their fellow-citizens. Backbiting and disunity, one-upmanship and flagrant immorality were rife. They clearly needed much more than a plain rebuke. Paul saw that their problem went far deeper: they had not appreciated the full impact of the cross. They were effectively interpreting it in the same way as the world around them, and so were not building their lives and lifestyles on what Jesus had done there. They did not seem able to accept the apparent failure of the cross because they were themselves so success-oriented. Now Paul had often experienced at first hand what it was like to tell people that he believed in a Saviour who died on a cross, only to see them immediately dismiss it. It was almost as if the Corinthians were doing the same thing, despite professing to be Christians. So it was vital to get through to them with the heart of the message of the cross. Paul persevered because he himself was convinced that at the cross there had been a victory. He knew that the true interpretation was that, when Christ died, he 'died for *our sins according to the Scriptures*' (1 Corinthians 15:3; my emphasis). Jesus' apparent failure was, in reality, his finest achievement.

A message that seems absurd

Who are the people you listen to? Who catches your imagination? Few trust politicians these days, few respect old institutions. Every major election stimulates the churning out of yet more opinion polls, and the 1999 Presidential Primaries in America were no exception. One woman who was polled remarked, 'That's all we need – another president!'[4] This sounds particularly ironic in the light of the debacle of the 2000 election wrangles between Al Gore and George W. Bush. The dead heat was widely interpreted as a lack of enthusiasm for either candidate. Cynicism about politics is rife on both sides of the Atlantic.

On top of that, current-affairs programmes tend to be dominated by 'experts'. Even they fail to arouse much interest, however, since for every one we hear, it is not hard to find three similarly qualified experts with contradictory opinions. If there are people to admire, they are often the protestors who stand on the boundaries shouting objections – the eco-warriors or the pop-star activists. Consequently, it is no surprise that the majority of people resign themselves to adopting opinions presented in the most convincing or polished way. Image is everything; what is *seen* carries arguments. Several films have brilliantly exposed the ease with which images can be doctored to communicate a specific message. The satirical *Wag the Dog* portrayed the antics of White House staff as they fabricate a Balkan War with the help of a Hollywood producer in order to divert attention from a presidential sex scandal. It was topical (to say the least), because at the time President Clinton was facing the Starr inquiry into the various scandals confronting him, while deploying American forces in the Balkans! In the film, images were deliberately manipulated to mask rather than reveal the truth.

Our age has incredible technological powers that even a few decades ago were inconceivable. They would, of course, have been entirely alien to the Corinthian world. The parallels between ancient Greek culture and ours are striking, nevertheless. You do not need a media-dominated world to be deceived by image or to avoid looking beneath the surface. This was precisely the phenomenon Paul experienced as he preached in the Greek world. The people held in highest esteem then were not so much the pop-music protestors as the market-place philosophers. They would hone their skills standing on soap-boxes, testing their views on any who would listen. A sizeable income could be earned if you tuned your message well enough, so some inevitably resorted to all kinds of rhetorical flourishes and devices to attract increasing numbers. Form and rhetoric quickly superseded content. This was all in the name of 'wisdom', of being able to make sense of the world. Complex systems of belief were touted around, into which people's experience of life would be squeezed. There were genuine and respectable orators around, of course, but marketplaces would also have seen their fair share of charlatans. Truth and reality were exchanged for mirages.

Where the form of an argument is more important than its content, a message about a saviour executed on a cross will *never* be attractive. There is nothing impressive about it at all. Consequently, whenever he preached it, Paul was on a collision course with Greek culture. He readily acknowledges this to the Corinthian Christians. He knew his message would never comply with worldly wisdom. 'For Christ did not send me to baptise, but to preach the gospel – not with words of human wisdom, lest the cross of Christ be emptied of its power. For the message of the cross is foolishness to those who are perishing, but to us who are being saved it is the power of God' (1 Corinthians 1:17–18).

One of the dominant, ancient Greek ideas was that the material world was tainted, even evil.[5] The spiritual world was all that mattered, because that alone was truly good. It does not take much imagination to see how the Christian claim that God became human in Jesus Christ in order to die on a cross then becomes totally untenable. As Paul says, 'it is foolishness' (verse 18). Now some, at that point, would despair of ever being able to get the message through. They might say that it is simply an instance of two incompatible belief systems existing side by side and leave it that. Paul cannot do that, because he sees what is happening beneath the surface. If you have as clear-cut a belief system as the Greeks did, then you have effectively determined how God must act. You have laid down parameters for what you can and cannot accept. God is not allowed to be the sovereign

God, absurd though that sounds. He is merely a cog in an intellectual wheel. God's response to this is devastating:

For it is written:

'I will destroy the wisdom of the wise;
the intelligence of the intelligent I will frustrate.'

Where is the wise man? Where is the scholar? Where is the philosopher of this age? Has not God made foolish the wisdom of the world?
(1 Corinthians 1:19–20, quoting Isaiah 29:14)

The Greeks were not unique in wanting to tell God what he should be like, however. Paul had realized that his fellow-Jews made exactly the same mistake: 'Jews demand miraculous signs and Greeks look for wisdom, but we preach Christ crucified: a stumbling-block to Jews and foolishness to Gentiles [i.e. all non-Jews]' (1 Corinthians 1:22–23). Jesus was asked to perform miracles throughout his ministry, and he demonstrated his astonishing ability to do amazing feats many times. On a number of occasions, however, he astonished everyone even more by *not* doing any. For instance, when the Pharisees asked him to perform for them, Jesus replied, 'A wicked and adulterous generation asks for a miraculous sign!' (Matthew 12:39). What was the problem? He didn't refuse parents of dying children, or blind men desperate to see. So why should he turn the Pharisees down?

The answer is simple. Jesus could penetrate façades. He knew that such demands demonstrate a desire to dictate terms to God. If God does this or that for me, then I will believe; the more spectacular the miracle, the better. If he doesn't, I won't. I am the arbiter. This makes God little more than a genie who responds to my every whim. Now, of course, Paul's fellow Jews would never have put it like that. They would no doubt have defended their challenges to Jesus on the grounds that the Messiah must establish his credentials through 'signs'. Nevertheless, they consistently failed to appreciate that God is God. He performs whatever signs he wants, whenever he wants. This means that his Messiah's greatest achievement might come through something that hardly looked like a miracle at all, if that was what God planned. It could even come through what appeared to be a complete contradiction in terms – crucifixion of the long-awaited Messiah. As we've already seen, for the Jewish mindset, that was unthinkable. And yet this was God's greatest achievement. In completing it, he proved that 'the foolishness of God is wiser than man's wisdom, and the weakness of God is stronger than man's strength' (1 Corinthians 1:25). Yes, the cross is going to be an inevitable problem for people who only recognize God in the spectacular or when he complies with their previously settled beliefs. It is a 'stumbling-block to Jews and foolishness to Gentiles' (1 Corinthians 1:23). That perfectly sums up the image of the cross.

We cannot leave this with the Jews and Greeks of Paul's day, however. Did you notice how Paul suddenly switches to using 'Gentiles' instead of 'Greeks' in verse 23? The original word literally means 'the nations'. The implication is clear. The cross is going to be a problem for *everyone*, whatever their philosophical or racial background. What seemed absurd to citizens of the Roman Empire in the first century is going to seem just as ridiculous now. An obvious question quickly follows, therefore. How does anyone *ever* believe in it?

The answer lies in whether or not we are able to accept God's verdict on all human beings. As we shall see, his charge against us is that we all sin. We all usurp God's rule over our lives, with far-reaching and devastating effects. Crucially for now, however, it means that we assume we are the centre of the world, and that God is not. Once we have made this shift, we inevitably try to force God to comply with our terms, whatever they might be. Consequently, we shall instantly dismiss the cross. It is just too ridiculous. The humiliation and defeat of the cross can have no place in the heart of those who have the arrogant audacity to assume they stand at the world's centre.

Do you see God's wisdom here? Part of his reason for working through the cross is precisely to force us to face reality. He wants us to confess in humility the appalling treason of taking his rightful place on the throne of our lives. Only after such an admission of guilt can we begin to be restored to him. We need to recognize that he alone is God. So only those with sufficient humility to acknowledge that their understanding is limited will have the humility to accept the cross. As Paul said, 'since in the wisdom of God the world through its wisdom did not know him, God was pleased through the foolishness of what was preached to save those who believe' (1 Corinthians 1:21). The cross humbles the proud, but it saves the humble. God is effectively saying, 'I'm going to do it in my own way, not yours', and so how we respond to the cross actually reveals our underlying attitude to God.

Yes, the cross does seem absurd. That was deliberate! It was God's express purpose to send his Son to die there. And the more we come to understand what happened there, the more we shall have our breath taken away by the greatest miracle God ever performed. Those who acknowledge it as the place where we are saved from our sin will recognize it as genuinely 'the power of God' (1 Corinthians 1:18). God has set the agenda for how he will act in his world, and for how he will rescue humanity from the effects of its sin. However, if the cross really is God's solution for sin, some major questions need to be addressed. What makes sin so serious? Why is a solution as extreme as the cross required? To these questions we shall turn our attention in part 2.

Summary
- The cross is at the very least an uncomfortable, if not obscene, religious symbol.
- Superficially, Jesus' death on a cross could hardly symbolize anything but failure. In reality, it marked his greatest victory.

- The cross breaks through our culture's complacent acceptance of the superficial and the trivial. It demonstrates God's awesome power and wisdom once and for all.

Part 2. Hard to accept, but hard to hide

3. United nations

Please read Romans 3:9–20 and Genesis 2:9 – 3:7

Even in the age of self-help websites, and 'fill-in-the-blank' templates, it is still unusual for people in their early twenties to write a will, but that is precisely what Cecil Rhodes did in 1877. After some canny investments in South African diamonds, he had become a multimillionaire at twenty-four. Drafting a will was therefore a sensible move for someone with wealth of that magnitude. He would of course live to become a central figure in the expansion of British rule in southern Africa, and would give his name to North and South Rhodesia (now Zambia and Zimbabwe). Those exploits were still ahead of him when he drafted his first will, but his ambitions knew no limits. The will had two executors: the Colonial Secretary back in London, and the regional Attorney General. It proposed the establishment of a secret society with the sole aim of bringing the whole planet under British control. That even included recovering the United States for the Empire! These days, that seems preposterous. At the time, it was not so fanciful. Britain was then easily the most powerful

nation in the world.[1] The real question, though, is what drove
Rhodes to such megalomania. The surprise is that it was his
theoretically wonderful ideals. His will stipulated that the society's
purpose was to establish 'so great a power as to hereafter render
wars impossible and promote the best interests in humanity'.[2]
How naive that sounds, how blind to the British Empire's own
shortcomings! The Empire could hardly claim to have established
a conflict-free environment in the areas under its control. What
hope was there for those still beyond its grasp?

The flaw, however, arguably lay not so much in Rhodes's ideals
as his belief that one single nation can attain them. That sort of view
was at least part of the motivation behind the creation of the United
Nations in 1945. The world had suffered intolerably as the result
of two world wars. Fifty-one countries united to prevent that
happening ever again, with others joining subsequently. The first
clause around which they united ran, 'We the peoples of the United
Nations determined to save succeeding generations from the
scourge of war, which twice in our lifetime has brought untold
sorrow to mankind.'[3] There can be little doubt that the UN has
contributed to world stability to some degree; nevertheless, in the
half-century since its foundation, inhumanity has relentlessly continued on every continent. Even during the opening years of the
twenty-first century, we have witnessed one conflict after another.
Why is it so hard for humanity to find peaceful unity? Why do the
ideals of the United Nations continue to lie beyond our grasp?

Many offer solutions and there are too many to list here;
but none ever seems to get to the root of the problem. Better
education is not a sufficient answer: although pre-Nazi Germany
was arguably one of the most highly educated and civilized
societies in the world, that did not prevent the Holocaust. Better
economic and political opportunities for all are not sufficient
either. Neither the great capitalist nor the communist experiments
of the twentieth century have eliminated conflict or inequality.
Only the Bible's answer seems to do justice to the gravity and the
extent of the predicament. Its consistent message is that sin lies at

the heart of the problem. It is an unfashionable and much misunderstood idea today but, once explained, its reality is hard to hide. A friend of mine, who has struggled with various doubts caused by a series of traumatic experiences, once said this to me: 'After all I've been through, I do struggle to believe certain aspects of the Christian message. But there is one thing of which I am absolutely certain: the reality of sin.'

A universal problem

Paul's letter to the Romans contains the Bible's longest and most sustained argument for the existence of sin. After almost three chapters, he asks, 'What shall we conclude then? Are we [Jews] any better? Not at all! We have already made the charge that Jews and Gentiles alike are all under sin' (Romans 3:9). The first part of his letter's argument would not have been controversial to his Jewish hearers. They needed little persuasion that Gentiles were sinners; it went without saying. The real controversy in Romans 2 and 3 was that Paul regarded his fellow-Jews as being on an equal footing with Gentiles. The Jews were God's chosen people; they had his law revealed to them; they therefore knew how to please him. Despite that, Paul maintains they did not please him. Having God's law may have given some advantages, but it did not keep them from sinning. They were ultimately no better off than the Gentiles were. Romans 3:9 is clear – both religious Jews and pagan Gentiles are implicated.

The controversy does not stop there. Paul consolidates his argument by quoting a string of verses from the Old Testament, which were of course the Jewish Scriptures.

As it is written:

'There is no-one righteous, not even one;
   there is no-one who understands,
   no-one who seeks God.
All have turned away ... '
(Romans 3:10–12)[4]

These Old Testament authors are unequivocal. They empha-size that the issue of sin is a universal problem and are clearly prepared to lump their fellow-Jews together with all humanity. They imply that sin primarily concerns not the extreme examples of human evil, such as murder and sexual abuse, but human-ity's deliberate rejection of God. This is why their astounding suggestion that religious people had actually 'turned away' from God was so controversial. Surely, they were precisely the people who did 'understand' and 'seek' him. We may not immediately see how this can be true; but it is not hard to see why it is offensive. Not only does it include those who are religious and those who are not; it implicitly incorporates all social and economic classes, all nationalities and cultures, all levels of civilization and sophistication. This is generalization in the extreme!

In the eighteenth century, the Countess of Huntingdon had a significant impact in England. She had become a Christian through the ministry of the renowned preacher George Whitefield and was one of his most enthusiastic supporters. Whenever she could, she would invite members of her social circle to hear him. One of these was the Dowager Duchess of Buckingham and this was her reply to one such invitation:

> I thank your ladyship for the information concerning the Methodist preachers.[5] Their doctrines are most repulsive and strongly tinctured with impertinence and disrespect before their superiors, in perpetually endeavouring to level all ranks and do away with all distinction. It is monstrous to be told you have a heart as sinful as the common wretches that crawl on the earth. This is highly offensive.[6]

It certainly was offensive; but does that make the doctrine false? The 'Methodist preachers' had not invented it. They were merely seeking to be faithful to the apostle Paul. That is why they were determined to preach it in the face of the inevitable offence it would give to 'their superiors'. Paul himself had anticipated precisely this sort of response but was still convinced of its truth. Sin is a universal problem. Strange though it may initially seem, *every* person in the world has turned away from God. That is the unequivocal claim of the Bible.

A pervasive reality

It is all very well to speak of the universality of sin, but how is this worked out? Can Paul sustain it at the personal level? Continuing in Romans 3, Paul pools more Old Testament passages to present his case. They make unpleasant reading.

'Their throats are open graves;
   their tongues practise deceit.'
'The poison of vipers is on their lips.'
   'Their mouths are full of cursing and bitterness.'
'Their feet are swift to shed blood;
   ruin and misery mark their ways,
and the way of peace they do not know.'
   'There is no fear of God before their eyes.'
(Romans 3:13–18)[7]

Paul is not trying to rub our noses in it for fun. He has a deliberate purpose. Before any disease can be treated, it must be fully diagnosed, and that diagnosis must be accepted by the patient. Paul has chosen his verses from the Old Testament with care. There is a deliberate progression from spoken words (Romans 3:13–14) to the lifestyle they so often manifest (Romans 3:15–17). It is vivid language; but these verses could so easily stand as a summary of the contents of the last week's news, let alone the last century's. Deceit has led to the shedding of blood, which all too often is innocent. So much of the world's suffering can be put down to the reality these verses describe. Just think of the experiences of ethnic minorities in the Balkans during the 1990s. Racial hatred was deceptively disguised by the good civil relations of people living side by side, but tragically manifested in genocide. That is extreme, of course, and yet the constant cry was that the crimes were perpetrated by 'ordinary' citizens, who killed people they had known since childhood.

Paul does not leave it hanging there. He sees a simple explanation for all this, taken this time from the prophet Isaiah: 'There is no fear of God before their eyes' (verse 18). He does not mean by 'fear' irrational anxiety, like being scared of the dark. The fear he refers to is the deep reverence and awe that inevitably come to those facing the true God. What the world lacks is deep conviction that God alone is God, and that we are his creatures. If we fully appreciated that, there would be no question of our trying to hold the moral high ground and believing that in God's eyes we must be doing 'quite well'. We would recognize how we have actually treated him.

It is easy to keep the implications of this at arm's length, but the Bible will not let us do that for long. It maintains that sin comes from the heart. After all, the deceit that pours from the mouth must come from somewhere. This is how Jesus himself put it: 'What comes out of a man is what makes him "unclean". For from within, out of men's hearts, come evil thoughts, sexual immorality, theft, murder, adultery, greed, malice, deceit, lewdness, envy, slander, arrogance and folly. All these evils come from inside and make a man "unclean" ' (Mark 7:20–23).

Jesus' list is not unique in the Bible, but it is perhaps the most comprehensive. He asserts that sin is not primarily an external force or an environmental pressure, but is heart-driven. The consequence is that every aspect of our being is affected. Sin affects our thinking and decision-making, our words and actions, and even our emotions and will. This has traditionally been called the doctrine of 'total depravity'. That title is perhaps misleading, since it does not mean that all human beings are as bad as they can possibly be. That would be palpably absurd, and would deny the fact that we remain creatures made in the image of God in spite of our sin. The doctrine simply states that 'no part of us is untouched by sin, and therefore no action is as good as it should be'.[8] When I realized how true this was of me, I think I took one of the most significant strides in my Christian life. It suddenly dawned on me how I actually enjoyed sinning. It was what I wanted to do. That came as quite a shock, but I could not escape its truth.

Such an admission does not come easily. We are quick to point to extenuating circumstances or other guilty parties. We even point at God, as we have already seen. How often do we examine our own lives to consider the trail we have left behind? The Christian thinker and writer Ravi Zacharias describes a meeting he had with one of America's most successful business-men on the top floor of his huge corporate building: 'Our entire conversation revolved around his question of so much evil in this world, and a seemingly silent God. Suddenly interrupting the conversation, a friend of mine said to him, "Since evil seems to trouble you so much, I would be curious to know what you have done about the evil you see within you." There was a red-faced silence.'[9]

The most surprising thing to some is the fact that even some of the world's most respectable and 'saintly' people would recognize Jesus' words as fair portraits of themselves:

> Dag Hammarskjöld, Secretary-General of the United Nations, a deeply committed public servant, [was] described by W. H. Auden as 'a great, good and lovable man'. But he had a very different opinion of himself. He bemoaned what he called 'that dark counter-centre of evil in our nature', and in particular the perversity which 'makes our unselfish service of others the foundation of our own self-esteem'.[10]

Or take the popular and highly acclaimed writer Somerset Maugham, who reputedly remarked that if he wrote down every thought he had ever thought and every deed he had ever done, he would be described as 'the monster of depravity'.

The Bible, then, not only teaches that sin is a universal problem, but also insists that it is an all-pervasive reality. There is a desperate irony here, however. Fifty years of UN influence have not brought peaceful unity to the world. Conflicts persist. And the Bible explains this by pointing to our deeper, underlying unity – our shared problem of sin. That is what makes the wonderful ideals of the UN ultimately impossible to achieve. What is happening on the international scale is merely an out-working of what happens on the personal scale.

How did this state of affairs come about? Is the reality of sin the fault of a Creator God or is there some other explanation for its origins? Once we have established the answer to that, we shall understand what lies behind Paul's Old Testament quotations. We shall be able to explain how religious people can be as sinful as non-religious people.

A common heritage

Many people dismiss Genesis out of court before they have even read it. The reason, very often, is that they forget or ignore that it was never designed to be a scientific manual. Its real purpose was instead to give a theological explanation for why the world is as it is. Consequently, it underpins the entire Bible. What it teaches, especially in the first three chapters, is fundamental to everything that follows it. That is no surprise – it deals with the creation of the universe! Genesis 3 gives a vivid and subtle picture of how things went wrong. This has led one commentator to say that 'Genesis 2 – 3, then, offers a paradigm of sin, a model of what happens whenever man disobeys God'.[11]

Chapters 1 and 2 of Genesis famously describe the origins of the universe. God created it with impressive order, wonderful diversity, and breathtaking perfection. Before he rested from his work, he created human beings who were uniquely made 'in his image'. Many people have filled those words with all kinds of speculation, but we must let the text itself guide our understanding. The least we can say is that God's image enabled human beings to relate to him and to one another, and to exercise great responsibilities in his world. 'So God created man in his own image, in the image of God he created him; male and female he created them. God blessed them and said to them, "Be fruitful and increase in number; fill the earth and subdue it"' (Genesis 1:27–28). This is an awesome statement of what we were created to be.

Adam and Eve therefore had an option: either to accept their God-given responsibilities or to reject them. Disobedience always had to be a tragic possibility. Otherwise, how could there be a genuine relationship of love between Creator and creature? That was what lay behind God's placing of a special tree in its garden home. This 'tree of the knowledge of good and evil' (Genesis 2:9) provided that possibility. God had said, 'You are free to eat from any tree in the garden; but you must not eat from the tree of the knowledge of good and evil, for when you eat of it you will surely die' (Genesis 2:16–17). The way Adam and Eve responded to this simple ban would reveal the true state of their relationship with God. Thus the scene is set for Genesis 3.

The existence of the serpent is never explained beyond the fact that he 'was more crafty than any of the wild animals the LORD God had made' (Genesis 3:1). There is certainly mystery here. There is no mystery, however, about his methods of enticing the man and woman (for both are clearly implicated in what happens). It is deeply subtle. All he does is ask a simple question: 'Did God really say, "You must not eat from any tree in the garden"?' It is subtle because, in one sense, there is nothing wrong in asking it, but in doing so, he encourages the woman to doubt her own understanding of what God had said. Notice also the implication that God is a killjoy. There is a deliberate distortion of what he said back in 2:17. The woman knows she cannot give a one-word reply – she must correct the misquotation; but when she does, she actually goes too far: 'We may eat fruit from the trees in the garden, but God did say, "You must not eat fruit from the tree that is in the middle of the garden, *and you*

must not touch it, or you will die" ' (Genesis 3:2–3; my emphasis).
God had never said anything about touching the fruit! One
distortion has led to another. By implication, God is mean and
restrictive.

Then comes the crunch. The serpent replies, 'You will not
surely die. For God knows that when you eat of it your eyes will
be opened, and you will be like God, knowing good and evil'
(Genesis 3:4–5). This is nothing other than a deliberate denial of
what God has said. More than that, it refutes God's assertion that
he will do anything about such flagrant disobedience. The serpent
promises a life of Godlike wisdom, a life that purports to improve
on the perfect life with God in his garden. But it is all mis-
information. The consequences of giving in to the temptation are
entirely negative. The promised enlightenment is a far cry from
the reality Adam and Eve will experience. They both eat, and their
eyes are opened. To their horror they taste not the ecstasy of new-
found, enlightened freedom, but crippling shame for their terrible
disobedience. Both are responsible to God, and both give in to the
temptation to disobey (Genesis 3:6–7).

So what made the fruit so attractive? In a documentary
reviewing her phenomenally successful and controversial pop
career, Madonna once suggested that the fruit of the tree was a
metaphor for sex. That explains what she sees as the Bible's
negative attitude to sex. The tabloid press seems to hold a similar
view, since sleaze and sex-scandal headlines invariably contain the
word 'sin'. These interpretations are both absurd and wrong.
Sexual intimacy was part of God's good creation plan, as can be
seen in Genesis 2:24–25. It has nothing whatsoever to do with the
serpent's temptation. The give-away phrase comes in 3:5 – 'you
will be like God'. There lies both the motivation and the
attraction. What precisely does that mean?

It all hinges on what the 'knowledge of good and evil' is.
Various suggestions have been offered. Some say it is simply
knowing that good and evil exist. This cannot be correct, since
they knew before that anything forbidden by God is by definition

evil. Perhaps it was a matter of experiencing evil. This does not fit either, since it is hard to see both the attraction in it and what is so Godlike about it. The most likely option is that 'knowing good and evil' concerns 'determining good and evil'. It is about seizing God's unique right to be able to say what is good and evil. Once that is achieved, I can be free to decide how I want to run my own life. I can be God in my own life and decide for myself what is right and wrong, without accountability to anyone else. In other words, the temptation of the tree appealed to their arrogant desire for autonomy, and autonomy is the essence of sin. We con ourselves into thinking that we are self-created, self-dependent and self-sustained. That interpretation explains why in Romans 3 Paul can talk about everyone turning away from God.

The chilling reality is that this can be done either respectably or flagrantly. You can write the rules of your own life in religious language, or in the language of the street. You can be a well-to-do executive from the suburbs or a shifty drug-pusher on the back streets; it makes no difference. God is still light-years away from the throne of your life. What is more, he is not conned by appearances, even if everyone else is. He knows your attitude all too well. Sin is essentially godlessness, which is not the same thing as atheism. It is about leaving the God who is there out in the cold. Adam's sin is something we have all inherited as his descendants. This is what lies behind Paul's statement in his letter to the Romans: 'sin entered the world through one man, and death through sin' (Romans 5:12). Just as the image of God is passed on from generation to generation,[12] so is sin. Many aspects of this are hard to fathom,[13] but we can see a parallel with our genes. Just as our genetic inheritance may give us various inclinations, so our inheritance of sin predisposes us towards self-determination. Sin's power is such that we all want to turn away from God and it is acting on that desire to rebel that is the real problem. The tragedy is that we choose our way instead of God's every time.

Despite some people's objections, we cannot disclaim responsibility for our sin on the grounds of inheritance, however. If we could, we would not therefore be able to take any credit for positive achievements in life either. In fact, that would make us mere programmed robots without responsibility or individuality, which is where the parallel with our genes is helpful. Take alcoholism, for example. Modern legal systems do in fact recognize that some people have a genetic predisposition towards alcoholism, but this does not diminish a drunken husband's responsibility in law if he beats up his wife. Alternatively, take Steve Redgrave's spectacular success at the 2000 Sydney Olympics, where he won his fifth consecutive rowing gold. He clearly had certain genetic predispositions that enabled him to become a brilliant rower. However, he still had to endure more than twenty years of sheer slog to achieve his success. He was a driven man with incredible will power and determination, and so it is entirely reasonable for him to take credit for what he has won. We are all happy to take credit for our achievements; how then can we deny responsibility for our failings (by appealing to 'nature' or 'nurture' or anything else)? We cannot have it both ways. So it is with our sin. We have inherited our sin from our parents. We are born biased, predisposed to live without God at the centre. Nevertheless, because that is precisely the way we want to live, we are responsible for it.

Does this not make sense of so much of what is wrong in our world? If people are trying to live as gods, conflict is inevitable. With everyone trying to be number one in their lives, someone has to come out on top. Friendships end and countries go to war. No-one is as bad as they can be because, despite our sin, we still retain God's image. Nevertheless, because of our sin, we are all far worse than we should be. Peaceful unity is impossible because of the very thing we all have in common. The nations truly are united, but united in their common rebellion against God. Before we can move on to considering how God views this reality, it is first necessary to assess what effects it has had on the world – the subject of the next chapter.

Summary
- Sin affects everyone.
- Sin affects every part of us, from our emotions, thought-life and will, to our words and actions.
- Sin gives us all an inherited desire to 'be like God' and live independently of our Creator.

4. Fatal addiction

Please re-read Genesis 3

The principal character in a powerful short story by Fay Weldon sits alone in a freezing church building on Good Friday. Lost in thought, she contemplates her life as an unhappily married art critic who has the power and influence to make or destroy careers. Uppermost in her mind is her brief affair with an artist she has profiled. Tragically, the affair led to the artist's wife committing suicide. The critic claims to feel no remorse for this. Reading the story, however, you cannot help but feel that she is suppressing it. Remorse would imply wrongdoing and that is the last thing she will admit. This is confirmed by her words near the start of the story. As she recounts her thoughts, she asks herself two significant questions: 'Everyone I meet believes they're good, does the best he or she can in the circumstances. But if everyone's good why is the world in such a state? And why should I not suffer from the same common delusion, that of my own goodness?'[1]

Thus, with that second question, she acknowledges that her claim to goodness is a 'delusion'. That is highly significant. She has deliberately persisted in her delusion, no doubt because that enables her to live with what has happened. Nevertheless, she seems to accept that it is still a delusion.

The Bible verifies what she acknowledges. John, in one of his letters, says, 'If we claim to be without sin, we deceive ourselves, and the truth is not in us' (1 John 1:8). It is of course no surprise that people do delude themselves, since admitting personal sin is galling and the incentives for not doing so are great. A delusion makes life seem more comfortable. Perhaps this explains why the Bible often describes not so much the roots of sin as its effects on our lives. It forces those who attempt to persist in their delusion to ask, 'In the light of these instantly recognizable realities, can I suppress the truth any longer?'

It promised so much ...
The great American lawyer Oliver Wendell Holmes once remarked, 'Sin has many tools, but a lie is the handle which fits them all.'[2] This was never truer than in the Garden of Eden, for, as we have seen, it was a blatant lie that lured the man and the woman into eating the fruit. The serpent alleged, 'You will not surely die' (Genesis 3:4). The enlightening prospect of becoming 'like God' was made all the more alluring by the promise of life without death. The serpent had no way of delivering the goods, however. His promise was built on quicksand. God had categorically stated that death would be the result of rejecting his authority. Not surprisingly, the consequences of believing the serpent's lie are both immense and horrendous. This truly was a fall from a great height.

The attraction of hard drugs makes a startling parallel here. When the actor John Belushi died of a cocaine and heroin overdose in 1983, one journalist described cocaine's seductive powers like this: 'It can do you no harm and it can drive you insane; it can give you status in society and it can wreck your career; it can make you the life of the party, and it can turn you into a loner; it can be an elixir for high living and a potion for death.'[3]

Indulging in drugs may seem harmless enough to begin with. It may even provide an entirely positive experience. But it is ultimately a deception. Reality soon kicks in, and it is sordid and lethal. Sin is like this; it seems so appealing and so liberating, but this appeal is based on a lie. The consequences are disastrous.

We are guilty

In Bernhard Schlink's novel *The Reader*, Hanna spends much of her adult life in prison as a convicted war criminal. She had committed a terrible atrocity as a Nazi prison guard, and there is no question as to her guilt; she is all too aware of it herself. The years of prison life have forced her to revisit her past many times. Here, we find her talking to her former lover, a man born after the war who is himself trying to come to terms with his whole nation's past:

> I always had the feeling that no one understood me anyway, that no one knew who I was and what made me do this or that. And you know, when no one understands you, then no one can call you to account. Not even the court could call me to account. But the dead can. They understand. They don't even have to have been there, but if they were, they understand even better. Here in prison they were with me a lot. They came every night, whether I wanted them or not.[4]

She is a woman tormented by her guilt. She has faced a dark reality, namely that we are most accountable to those we have harmed or abused. In her case, the offended parties all died in the burning church that she and the other guards had deliberately left locked. Her victims return to haunt her dreams, for they are the ones who can hold her accountable.

As the one we have all offended, God is similarly in a position to hold us to account. This is how Paul puts it. He has explained that both Jews (who have the privilege of possessing God's revealed moral standard or law) and Gentiles (who do not) are equally sinful, as we saw in the previous chapter. Now he concludes this whole section in Romans with a summary of humanity's predicament: 'Now we know that whatever the law says, it says to those who are under the law, so that every mouth may be silenced and the whole world held accountable to God. Therefore no-one will be declared righteous in his sight by observing the law; rather, through the law we become conscious of sin' (Romans 3:19–20).

Paul leads those of us who would put God in the dock into God's celestial courtroom. When those who know the perfect standard of God's law are measured up against it, even they are left speechless. They know they have not been 'righteous', in a right relationship with God. The law is not some external code to which God is bound, but an expression of his very character and nature. When confronted by that, there is 'consciousness of sin', an awareness both of how far they fall short of God's perfection and how much they have offended him. The law could never make anyone righteous – its standard is simply too high. So if those who have the law are unable to be righteous, what hope is there for those that do not have the law? They are unable to keep their own standards, let alone God's. All humanity therefore stands guilty as charged. 'Every mouth is silenced', not because they have exploited the right to remain silent, but because they have nothing to say – there is no defence to bring.

God is uniquely in a position to bring these charges against us. As our Creator, he alone can legitimately hold us all account-able. As our rightful Lord, he alone is the one we have all offended. He is the one we have sought to usurp. He is the one we have tried to evade. Who can deny that this guilt is genuine?

Some commentators today are claiming that we should avoid the idea of guilt altogether. They say it is no longer relevant, because our society is not what is called a 'guilt culture'. Is that necessarily the case, however? A sense of guilt may not of course be the first problem people want solving when we talk with them, but there is no denying that it is a genuine issue for many. A psychiatrist once remarked that if he could convince his patients that their sins were forgiven, 75% of them would walk away the next day without need for further help. You don't have to be suffering from mental illness to want forgiveness, however. In his intriguingly titled book *The Sane Society*, Erich Fromm wrote, 'It is indeed amazing that in as fundamentally an irreligious culture as ours, the sense of guilt should be so widespread and deeprooted as it is.'[5] We all have skeletons in the cupboard. The truth is, however, that whether or not we *feel* guilty, we cannot hide the fact that we *are* guilty. Wisdom may dictate that we don't use a sense of guilt as a 'way in' to talking about Christian truth, but we cannot do justice to God and the cross without it. We all stand before him helplessly guilty.

Oscar Wilde drives this home brilliantly in his play *An Ideal Husband*. One of the principal characters, Sir Robert Chiltern, is a promising Member of Parliament who, years before, had made some deeply compromising business deals. An old acquaintance tries to blackmail him, and during the course of their conversation, she remarks, 'Even you are not rich enough, Sir Robert, to buy back your past. No man is.'[6] That is profoundly true. Even if each of us were able to turn a completely new leaf, and live a perfect life from this point on, we should never be able to eradicate our past. Who has nothing to regret? Who has nothing to be ashamed of? Above all, who can claim always to have lived for God? Certainly not this writer.

Unfortunately, the consequences of our sin do not stop there.

We are alienated
Adam and Eve's instinctive reaction after eating the fruit was to run. That is a normal reaction to a sense of guilt, isn't it? 'Then the man and his wife heard the sound of the LORD God as he was walking in the garden in the cool of the day, and they hid from the LORD God among the trees of the garden' (Genesis 3:8).

This is the first indication of the seriousness of the disaster. They were running from the God to whom they owed everything: from their incredible environment to their very existence; from the provision of their relationship with each other to their awesome privileges and responsibilities in the Garden. Now they wanted to hide. Their former intimacy with God had degenerated into evasion tactics and skulking in the undergrowth. Shame had clearly driven them to this, but no doubt so had the gradual realization that their decision to try to become 'like God' must lead to conflict with him. There is a terrible poignancy about God's questions: 'Where are you? . . . Who told you that you were naked? Have you eaten from the tree from which I commanded you not to eat?' (Genesis 3:9, 11). Of course, he knew full well what their answers would be, but the fact that he asked them at all serves to reveal his deep disappointment and sadness.

Their alienation from God did not stop there. It was made physical when God had to banish them from the Garden:

> And the LORD God said, 'The man has now become like one of us, knowing good and evil. He must not be allowed to reach out his hand and take also from the tree of life and eat, and live for ever.' So the LORD God banished him from the Garden of Eden to work the ground from which he had been taken. After he drove the man out, he placed on the east side of the Garden of Eden cherubim and a flaming sword flashing back and forth to guard the way to the tree of life.
> (Genesis 3:22–24)

This physical banishment merely confirms the deep chasm that had arisen between humanity (which has sought to be 'like God') and the one who alone is truly God. There appeared to be no hope of return. From this point onwards every human being is born 'east of Eden', outside the Garden, without intimacy with the living God. The tragedy is that our sin makes us want to remain outside – for we ourselves believe the lie that to be free from God's rule brings actual freedom. We relish the chance to call the shots in our own lives, even believing that such freedom increases our long-term enjoyment of life. That is a delusion. If you have ever experienced that sense of prayers bouncing off the ceiling, this is the root cause. Our sin alienates us from the God to whom we owe everything.

Inevitably, this alienation affects everything else in God's world. For a start, there is a deep alienation between humanity and the creation we were designed to protect. Having rejected the Creator's blueprint for how creation should be ordered, humanity now faces conflict with the environment. The fall brings enmity between the woman and the serpent (Genesis 3:15), and sweat and toil to working the land (Genesis 3:17–18). It also brings danger. Bizarre though it initially seems, this alienation from the natural world can therefore be seen every time we hear of natural disasters and tragedies. Despite its innumerable wonders, the natural world contains huge terrors. As I write, countless thousands have been overwhelmed by the flooding of the Limpopo River in Mozambique. News cameras have captured images of pregnant mothers and frail grandfathers desperately clinging to treetops, surrounded by mile after mile of swelling water. A world that was created to be the perfect environment for us to inhabit now persistently threatens our very existence. The Bible maintains that the root cause for this is not a flaw in God's design, but what happened in the Garden. One commentator puts it like this: 'Since humanity is the dominant species on earth, human sin is bound to have very widespread effects on nature as a whole. The Fall disturbed humanity's harmonious relationship with nature, alienating us from nature, so that we now experience nature as hostile, and introducing elements of struggle and violence into our relationship with nature.'[7] This fundamental dislocation means that even those natural phenomena which have nothing ostensibly to do with human activity can be seen as consequences of the fall.

More immediate evidence for our fundamental alienation can be seen at the personal level. The 'sex war' began at the eating of the fruit. Both the man and the woman tried to shift the blame away from themselves (Genesis 3:12–13). Where there should have been mutual support and care, the relationship between Adam and Eve had soured. They now had a consuming desire for self-preservation, a craving at the root of so many of the problems we can see in our world even now. Within one generation of the fall, personal conflict led to its inevitable conclusion – Cain murdered his brother Abel (Genesis 4). It illustrates that after this primal sin there can be no such thing as the perfect relationship. Conflict inevitably rears its head, with a sense of isolation often the result. This hardly needs illustrating, since we can see this in our own daily lives. Even the best friendships are spoiled by the pain of arguments and selfish preoccupations.

Is this not one of the root causes for the acute first-year loneliness suffered by a sixth of all British university students?[8] They feel excluded by peers and course-mates to the extent that a proportion take the drastic step of leaving university altogether. What should be an enlightening and life-changing time leaves the bitter taste of isolation. Or take an even more distressing example: racism. Arthur Ashe was a great tennis player, who died tragically after contracting Aids from a blood transfusion. A mild-mannered and greatly admired man, he said this as he looked into the eyes of reporters who had gathered for his first public acknowledgment of his illness: 'Painful though it is to know that I have this dread disease, nothing could be as painful as the rejection I have endured all my life by virtue of my colour.'[9] There is a terrible irrationality about racism. At its heart lies the fear of anyone who is different, because (for whatever reason) he or she threatens our concern for self-preservation. This causes intolerable agony, isolation and loneliness.

Just pick up today's newspaper. The alienating effect of sin is visible on every front page because it manifests itself in every aspect of our lives. This is how the apostle Paul describes his world: 'We lived in malice and envy, being hated and hating one another' (Titus 3:3). Are things so different now? Do we not see all around us mutual hostility, people wishing evil on other people, and people resenting the good things enjoyed by other people? Relationships are not always marked by these things, but who can claim never to have felt envy or malice? Alienation runs deep.

We are enslaved

Intriguingly, that verse in Paul's letter to Titus begins, 'At one time we too were foolish, disobedient, deceived and enslaved by all kinds of passions and pleasures' (Titus 3:3). Note how he includes himself. There is no sense of his claiming the moral high ground here. Nor should we forget that his former career was as a highly respected Jewish leader, a Pharisee, whose lifestyle many regarded as the epitome of moral rectitude. And still he describes himself as 'enslaved'.

There is an account of a wealthy building contractor who was involved in the construction of the rather disconcertingly named Tombs Prison in New York. Not long after its completion he was found guilty of forgery and sentenced to several years in the prison he had built. As he was escorted into a cell of his own making, he remarked to the prison officer, 'I never dreamed when I built this place that I would one day be an inmate.' This is profoundly true of sin. Our desires imprison us. We become mastered by the very thing we assume we can control. In a genuine sense, sin is therefore an addiction. We cannot give it up, despite the terrible damage it inflicts.

This does not take long to prove. We don't even need the benchmark of God's revealed morality to prove it. We merely have to attempt to live up to our own standards to discover the impossibility of breaking our addiction by ourselves. Paul summed the situation up brilliantly from his own experience: 'For what I do is not the good I want to do; no, the evil I do not want to do – this I keep on doing' (Romans 7:19). He goes on to say that this makes him 'a prisoner of the law of sin at work within my members' (Romans 7:23). So we could even describe this consequence of the fall as alienation within us. There is a dislocation and therefore a struggle between our conscience and our mind. Our conscience informs us that we ought to take a particular course of action; our mind decides that we would rather do something else, very often for our own sake rather than for others. We are enslaved by what we want, which is ultimately independence from our Creator. Just test any recent decision: Whose interests were you dominated by? Your own, or God's? If that is not sufficient proof, determine to keep the Ten Command- ments (in Exodus 20) perfectly for just twenty-four hours and then be scrupulously honest about measuring up your thoughts, as well as your words and deeds. Do you need any further proof of the truth of our enslavement?

We are defiled

It is common to hear the victims of crime describing their experience in terms of dirtiness or defilement. Burglary victims often feel disturbed out of all proportion to what has been stolen, because their privacy has been invaded. Their rooms don't look the same, with the knowledge that an anonymous intruder has rifled through them. The sense of defilement is even more understandable after a rape, where the nature of the crime was a more fundamental violation.

The Bible takes this idea further, since it teaches that sin also defiles those who commit the sin. Jesus made this clear in a debate with some scholars. The Old Testament had much to say about ritual defilement, detailing how uncleanness came from contact with all kinds of things, such as dead bodies, certain foods and infectious diseases.[10] This ritual defilement meant that the affected person became unfit for the presence of God. The only hope for readmission was to undergo ritual cleansing. What Jesus' con- temporaries failed to appreciate, however, was the deeper reality that this was always intended to represent. They seemed con- cerned only with external defilement; Jesus was not, as we saw in the previous chapter: 'What comes out of a man is what makes him "unclean" ... All these evils come from inside and make a man "unclean"' (Mark 7:20, 23). The very thing that enslaves us, therefore, both damages us deeply and makes us unfit for the presence of God.

That sin damages the sinner will come as no surprise. The poet Byron summarized the anguish of this brilliantly. He was a man who could euphemistically be described as having lived a 'full and varied' life, which makes all the more likely the possibility that the following words were in some way autobiographical:

> The thorns I have reaped are of the tree
> I planted, – they have torn me, and I bleed:
> I should have known what fruit would spring
>   from such a seed.[11]

This damage leaves indelible marks. Just as we are unable to expunge our guilt for our past, so are we unable to wipe this defilement away. We are like Shakespeare's Lady Macbeth after her part in the murder of King Duncan. She sleepwalks along the castle corridors, desperately trying to rub the king's imaginary blood from her hands. All incriminating traces of the king's real blood had of course been washed away before, but her conscience is tormented by the deeper reality of her remaining defiled by her deed. No amount of soap and water can change that.

Why this defilement makes us unfit for God's presence is perhaps harder to grasp. If you have seen the film *Blade Runner*, then you will remember that disturbing scene when Roy Batty, the state-of-the-art android with a pre-programmed lifespan, forces his way into the private apartment of his ingenious creator, Tyrell. He has only one demand – more life. His creator is his last hope for reprogramming, but when he is spurned, the consequences are tragic for both Tyrell and Batty. In our conceit, we assume that we can do something similar: barge into God's presence to make our own demands. All the time, however, we forget what our sin has done to us. Our defilement means that we do not stand a chance in the presence of a holy God – just like an old bunch of flowers thrown into an industrial furnace.

Imagine a great Old Master painting in the National Gallery. It is an object of incredible beauty, and visitors file past it open-mouthed at its detail and colours. Its characters almost seem alive, as if blood really is coursing through their veins. Suppose a vandal attacks it with spray paint and a knife. It is ruined and no longer fit for public viewing. Tragically, gallery staff have no choice but to remove it and place it in a storeroom. You could say that it has been defiled, and to keep it on display would be an affront to its painter. It has lost all its former glory. Similarly, God has no choice but to remove us from his presence. Defilement necessitates banishment, just as Adam and Eve first experienced in Genesis 3. In the next chapter we shall consider in greater detail why this follows. For now, we can appreciate why some people sense they are unfit for God.

... But God's promise proves true

Paul wrote that 'the wages of sin is death' (Romans 6:23). There is nothing particularly revolutionary about this statement. What God promised back in the Garden as the consequence of disobeying him simply came true. Sin irresistibly leads to death, because that is how God 'wired up' his creation. Paul's illustration of a wage conveys the idea of just deserts. As he explained a couple of chapters before, 'when a man works, his wages are not credited to him as a gift, but as an obligation' (Romans 4:4). In other words, this is what he earns. He would be hard done by if he did not receive his wages. Similarly, sin earns death, as each of its consequences leads to this. For instance, to be guilty of rejecting God makes us stand justly condemned and therefore liable to getting as a punishment what we ask for. Placing ourselves on God's throne effectively alienates us from the one who rightfully occupies that throne, the very God who created and sustains life itself. To be enslaved to, and therefore defiled by, sin means that we are unfit for the presence of God. All four consequences lead to certain death.

One problem remains with this. Think back to the fateful day of Adam and Eve's eviction from God's presence. This is speculative of course, but they might well have assumed they had escaped lightly. They had initially survived their eviction, hadn't they? They were still alive! Perhaps the serpent had been right after all. The writer of Genesis knows what he is doing, however. Through their banishment from God's presence in the Garden, they actually died spiritually; that is the greatest tragedy of the fall. Their spiritual intimacy with their Creator was destroyed, which is why Gordon Wenham can describe their expulsion from God's presence as 'a living death ... [which] was yet more catastrophic than physical death'.[12] For as Henri Blocher puts it, 'In the Bible, death is the reverse of life – it is not the reverse of existence. To die does not mean to cease to be, but in biblical terms it means "cut off from the land of the living", henceforth unable to act, and to enter another condition.'[13]

This is not to say that this spiritual death lacks physical consequences. Within just two chapters, the full experience of physical death becomes a reality as well. Genesis 4 describes the first death, the result of violence; Genesis 5 contains a long and, at first sight, uninspiring genealogy – uninspiring, that is, until we notice its constant refrain. Over and over the writer repeats the simple words 'and then he died'.[14] It is like a drumbeat – a drumbeat of death. This was not the way the world was meant to be – but it was the inevitable consequence of sin. We try to take on God's role, but inevitably we fail. Death is the result.

This explains why suffering and death are so alien to us. Whenever death comes, it brings pain and anguish. It is an unnatural intrusion into life, causing fear and despair. This is true even in the case of terminal illness, where death seems both inevitable and a relief. There is still loss and grief. The Roman historian Pliny remarked two millennia ago that death is always premature. It is more than that, however; it is cruel, appearing to render life meaningless. As the great Russian writer Leo Tolstoy put it, 'Is there any meaning in my life that will not be annihilated by the inevitability of death that awaits me?'[15]

Death was not what we were made for; but when we sin, it is what we ask for.

Summary

This table makes all too clear the desperate extent of our need. Given this predicament, and given the offence we cause to God, how can we ever escape the consequences of our sin?

Sin's effects	What sin leads to	What we need
We are guilty		to be *forgiven*
We are alienated		to be *reconciled*
We are enslaved	**DEATH**	to be *liberated*
We are defiled		to be *cleansed*
	⟶	to be given *life*

5. Divine justice

Please read Isaiah 6 and Romans 1:18 – 2:6

If you become engaged to be married, you inevitably find yourself faced with a huge list of things to do. At the top of it is the question of the ring. Imagine you set out to buy a ring with a beautiful single-diamond setting. The jeweller will want to show it off in its best light, which is why a common practice is to roll out a piece of very dark cloth on the counter. Once set against this contrasting background, the diamond sparkles brilliantly. Previously unimagined colours and depths to the gem suddenly appear.

Jesus' death on the cross is a little like that diamond. It amazes and confounds us. Taken out of context, however, it is impossible to grasp its awesome significance. It needs that dark cloth behind it. Only then will it sparkle in all its brilliance. We have already considered aspects of that background in the previous chapters, namely our sin and its consequences. We must take it one stage further, however, for the news must appear to get worse before it can get better. There must be more discomfort before we can draw true comfort from Jesus' death. Only then shall we realize how thrilling and breathtaking it really is. The final piece in the jigsaw before we can come to the good news is how God reacts to our sin. The Bible is adamant that if he is to be true to himself, God must judge it. The question is, 'Why?'

The holiness of God

The Jewish prophet Isaiah had the unenviable task of declaring an uncompromising message. He lived and worked in Jerusalem over a period of at least forty years, beginning towards the end of King Uzziah's reign (around 740 BC). The first five chapters of his book set the scene by exposing the period's true character. Exploitation and oppression of the powerless were rampant (Isaiah 1:21–23). Unfaithfulness to the God who had rescued them from Egypt was unbridled (Isaiah 1:2–4; 2:6–8). Society was in turmoil (Isaiah 5:7). But then it got personal for Isaiah; the big picture was not enough. He was forced to recall his own confrontation with God, the God in whose name he had been called to speak:

> In the year that King Uzziah died, I saw the Lord seated on a throne, high and exalted, and the train of his robe filled the temple. Above him were seraphs [heavenly servants of God], each with six wings: With two wings they covered their faces, with two they covered their feet, and with two they were flying. And they were calling to one another:
>
> > 'Holy, holy, holy is the LORD Almighty;
> > the whole earth is full of his glory.'
>
> At the sound of their voices the doorposts and thresholds shook and the temple was filled with smoke.
> (Isaiah 6:1–4)

It was highly unusual for a prophet to date the start of his ministry with a death. He could so easily have introduced the chapter with 'in the year that Jotham became king'. The probable reason is that Uzziah's dying months were symbolic of the general state of the nation. The contrast with Israel's heavenly king could not have been greater. Notice how Isaiah describes his vision. He never actually saw God face to face, for he is far too 'high and exalted'. He was out of sight. The 'train of his robe' was all that was needed to fill the temple. Isaiah did witness the constant activity that surrounded the throne, however, as heavenly beings went about the business of serving and praising God. Nevertheless, what stands out most in his vision is not what he saw, but what he heard: the angelic seraphs' song.

The way to express the totality or excellence of something in Old Testament Hebrew was simply to repeat the word. For example, when the writer of Genesis wanted to say that a particular place was 'full of tar pits' (Genesis 14:10) he described it (literally) as 'pits pits'. Repetition was used to make the point. The seraphs in Isaiah's vision repeat 'Holy *three* times! This is the only occasion in Hebrew literature where this happens, thus giving God's holiness unique emphasis. As Alec Motyer puts it, God's 'holiness is in itself so far beyond human thought that a "super-superlative" has to be invented to express it'.[1] So what is so special about God's holiness that warrants this special treatment? What does it mean for him to be 'holy'?

Mention 'holiness' to most people and images of monks in habits or supposedly pious churchgoers immediately spring to mind. Those sorts of pictures do not tend to generate a sense of awe! In fact, anyone who appears 'holier than thou' is usually treated with the contempt they deserve. Holiness seems neither awe-inspiring nor terrifying; and yet when Isaiah had his vision, God's holiness was unquestionably both these things. Why else would he react like this? ' "Woe to me!" I cried. "I am ruined! For I am a man of unclean lips, and I live among a people of unclean lips, and my eyes have seen the King, the LORD Almighty" ' (Isaiah 6:5).

Having glimpsed God's glory, Isaiah was immediately confronted by his own sin. That his 'unclean lips' were the first things to come to mind is no surprise. Preaching was his profession, so his lips were in some ways representative of his whole life. In total contrast to the holiness of God, he stood fully exposed. 'I am ruined!' he cried. It is as if he had been cross-examined without God even having to say a word. He suddenly became aware that his presence before a holy God put him at great personal risk. He knew that he was as incriminated as those to whom he would preach. Isaiah was not unique in this, of course. Job and the prophet Ezekiel also realized their unworthiness when God confronted them (Job 42:6; Ezekiel 1:28), as did those in the New Testament who glimpsed Jesus' true identity. So after the miraculous catch of fish, Peter asked Jesus to 'Go away from me, Lord; I am a sinful man' (Luke 5:8). Then after his vision of Jesus in heaven, John 'fell at his feet as though dead' (Revelation 1:17). The Bible repeatedly emphasizes God's holiness.

Holiness has been defined as 'everything about God that sets him apart from us and makes him an object of awe, adoration, and dread to us'.[2] Central to this holiness is his moral purity and perfection. He is white hot in his purity, which is why the presence of God is so often associated with fire and smoke in the Bible. Just as a burning building is impossible to enter, even for rescue workers in protective gear, so God is totally unapproachable. The prophet Habakkuk put it like this:

Your eyes are too pure to look on evil;
    you cannot tolerate wrong.
(Habakkuk 1:13)

Isaiah's vision takes us further. Did you notice how the seraphs had to cover their faces (Isaiah 6:2)? We can assume that, as heavenly servants of God, they were not evil at all; and yet God's holiness required even seraphs to cover their eyes.

The holiness of God manifests itself in a number of ways, but we shall focus on two: his justice and his wrath. These are not immediately attractive or popular ideas today, but we must persevere with them. If we try to downplay either of them, we end up in a far more frightening situation than if we hold on to them. For the truth is that we actually *need* God's justice and wrath. Indeed, these are crucial elements in what makes the Christian message fundamentally *good* news. I remember a conversation with a close Congolese friend after he had suffered terrible trauma and consequently had to flee to Uganda as a refugee. He has thankfully now been resettled to Australia; but at the time, he put it this way: 'Without the knowledge that justice and judgment are coming, I would never be able to trust that God is good!'

The justice of God

One of the reasons people find this such a jarring idea is that the God of the New Testament is described as loving. In fact, John categorically states that 'God is love' (1 John 4:16). Where does this fit with all the talk of wrath and justice? Many assume that it cannot. This conclusion is then fuelled by the enduring misapprehension that the Old Testament presents a God of wrathful justice, while the New Testament counteracts this with the God of love. This is plainly false. The Old Testament is full of passages revelling in God's love (for example: Numbers 14:17–20; Deuteronomy 7:7–10; Psalms 103; 118:1–3; Hosea 11:1–11), while Jesus himself taught about judgment and hell as much as, if not more than, anyone else in the Bible (for example: Matthew 23:1 – 25:46; Mark 8:35–38; Luke 13:1–5; John 5:24–30). The inescapable reality is that the New Testament reveals both God's love and his wrath more clearly than the Old. The stereotypes simply do not fit. So where do we go from here?

We must start by recognizing two common mistakes. The first is the absurd assumption that God's nature can be reduced to a single word or concept. The current vogue is to do this with his love, as if John's statement that God is love was all that could be said about him. It is simply not possible to do that to the infinite God revealed in the Bible. The second mistake is to assume that love and justice are incompatible. There are tensions between them, certainly, but to say they are incompatible is plainly not true. As we shall discover, the cross is where God's justice and his love are perfectly expressed together in a single act. We do not need to resort to the cross to understand this, however. Even at the human level, our love for people will mean that we want the best for them. That will sometimes lead to anger and a righting of wrongs, because the opposite of love is not anger, but indifference. To say 'I don't really care' is tantamount to saying 'I don't love you'. Anger and love are often two sides of the same coin.

A constant whine almost from the day we started talking was, 'Mum/Dad, that's not fair.' The slightest whiff of parental inconsistency, or of a brother or sister receiving preferential treatment, caused screams and tantrums. The aim was to continue screaming until our demands were met (if exhaustion did not intervene first). If we had the advantage, we of course kept quiet. The last thing we wanted was to have to share that extra packet of sweets in our pocket, but that is another story! Everyone who suffers injustice in any form feels it keenly. Then, when others suffer it, we cannot fail to be moved by their plight. The television news regularly fills our living rooms with images of despairing refugees, swindled pensioners and abused children. 'That is not fair!' we cry. 'How could it happen? Why can't "they" do something, whoever "they" are?'

This is, of course, what we considered in the introductory chapter. These are precisely the questions we want God to answer because we *need* him to be just. If this is not our experience, the most likely explanation is that we have not suffered much injustice personally. If we had, we would be craving for God's justice. That is why Habakkuk goes on to say in the verse already quoted:

> Your eyes are too pure to look on evil;
>> you cannot tolerate wrong.
> Why then do you tolerate the treacherous?
>> Why are you silent while the wicked
>> swallow up those more righteous than themselves?
> (Habakkuk 1:13)

Far from finding God's justice unpalatable, Habakkuk's greatest fear was that God's justice was unreliable. The fact that the perpetrators of evil seemed to be getting away with it threw all his old confidence into turmoil. Evil cannot be brushed under the carpet. It must be exposed for what it is and then dealt with.

Pol Pot's regime in Cambodia was one of the most terrifying and bloody the world has ever seen. Just over a third of the country's entire population died.[3] The Khmer Rouge systematically set about destroying anything to do with love and friendship, family life and religion.[4] Bernard Levin made this poignant comment only twelve months after Pol Pot's revolution:

> Cambodia has achieved a distinction which has so far eluded even those countries unfortunate enough to experience the full weight of terror brought to bear by even the most monstrous tyrants of our time; it is the first country to be transformed into a concentration camp in its entirety ... in Cambodia, ignored by the outside world, the unburied dead cry for vengeance, and the living dead for pity; and cry, both, in vain.[5]

Evil like that must be exposed. It cries out for justice. How can anyone dispute this? To think otherwise is an offence. Some try to rationalize this, or to claim that there has been gross exaggeration. You cannot play fast and loose with historical evidence in order to cover up evil, however, which explains the bitter antagonism towards British historian David Irving in April 2000. He was branded by a High Court judge as a 'Holocaust denier, falsifier of history and racist' because he refused to accept the Nazis' systematic extermination of Jews. His claim was that 'more people died in the back of Kennedy's car at Chappaquiddick than died in the gas chambers at Auschwitz'.[6] That is a sickening assertion. Evil will not go away simply because we try to hide it or explain it away; nor will it if we rebrand evil with a more palatable word: 'Words are not puffs of air. We cannot rename wickedness and consider it solved. There is an irrepressible voice, and it is the voice of the soul, which says evil cannot be trivialised.'[7]

The Bible is utterly consistent about this. God is just and he will do something about evil. God's justice is good news because, in all reality, millions around the globe are unlikely to find satisfactory justice in a human court of law. As we shall discover, the fact that Jesus had to die on the cross to deal with our sin proves categorically that God does not trivialize evil. Centuries before, however, Isaiah himself was confident that God's justice would prevail:

> So man will be brought low
>   and mankind humbled,
>   the eyes of the arrogant humbled.
> But the LORD Almighty will be exalted by his justice,
>   and the holy God will show himself holy by his righteousness.
> (Isaiah 5:15–16)

The difficulty, though, is where to find the evidence for this justice. The experiences of people all around surely lead us to echo Habakkuk's confused cry rather than Isaiah's confident statement of faith:

> Why then do you tolerate the treacherous?
>   Why are you silent while the wicked
>   swallow up those more righteous than themselves?
> (Habakkuk 1:13)

The wrath of God
Anger by itself is neutral, and it can be a necessary and positive reaction to terrible evil. How could we have seen something of the plight of Cambodia, for instance, without being moved to anger? Anger can also be totally unreasonable. Human beings are often provoked to anger by the most trivial things. A stubbed toe, for instance, can make us lash out at the nearest person for no just

reason. As one ancient writer, Cato, once said, 'An angry man opens his mouth, and closes his eyes.' Our anger makes us blind, which gives anger a bad name and is especially dangerous when we attribute anger to God. We too easily assume that his anger is equally unreasonable or unpredictable. After all, some of the pagan gods worshipped at the time of Jesus were certainly like that. The Greek king of the Gods, Zeus, was prone to throwing a thunderbolt down on some unsuspecting mortal whenever his whim led him. Is the God of the Bible like that? If he is, it is particularly worrying to discover that the Old Testament uses twenty words for God's anger or wrath, and contains 580 references to it.[8] Fortunately, he is not like Zeus at all; his anger is revealed certainly, but not as a sudden bolt from the blue. This is how Paul puts it: 'The wrath of God is being revealed from heaven against all the godlessness and wickedness of men who suppress the truth by their wickedness, since what may be known about God is plain to them, because God has made it plain to them' (Romans 1:18–19).

The wrath referred to here is not irrational; it is the outworking of his holiness, which cannot endure evil. It is 'his active judicial hostility to sin' and as such 'is wholly just in its manifestations'.[9] It condemns only what is evil (because it must), and is never random or whimsical. What is more, this is entirely consistent with a God of love.

For three weeks in April and May 1999, Londoners were held in anxious suspense by a series of nail bombs in the heart of the city. These were targeted at specific areas frequented by different minority groups. The first, on 18 April, went off in a shopping centre in the Afro-Caribbean area of Brixton. The second, a week later, went off in the heart of the Asian community in Brick Lane. The third killed three and injured sixty-five in a gay pub in Soho. Within a day of that blast, David Copeland was arrested and charged with the bombings. His father Stephen found himself having to make a press statement about the accusations brought against his son: 'Myself and my family totally condemn the cowardly and barbaric bombings carried out in London in the last two weeks. If David is guilty of these awful acts of violence then we also totally condemn him for carrying them out. Until all the facts are known, we cannot say anything further.'[10]

We have no idea of the quality of their relationship, and yet would anyone with even the strongest feelings of paternal affection be able to say anything else? The evil had to be faced. That condemnation of his son did not deny his love, nor would a call for his crimes to be punished. The real test for the depth of that love would come in how the relationship progressed once the condemnation had been made. In itself, the condemnation is not the issue. It is no different when it comes to God, who can condemn and still be true to his character of love. What is different is that his condemnation is announced to the world not through a press statement, but in two principal ways.

In the present

After some grim examples of God's wrath being meted out in the present (Romans 1:21–27), Paul sums up his point: 'since they did not think it worth while to retain the knowledge of God, he gave them over to a depraved mind, to do what ought not to be done' (Romans 1:28).

Paul repeats that chilling phrase 'God gave them over' three times in this section (Romans 1:24, 26, 28). He is effectively saying, 'Don't look for God's wrath in thunderbolts from heaven. Just because you think you've escaped being "struck down" for your misdemeanours, don't think you're not being judged for them. God judges through the consequences of people's sin.' You may have gained the impression from the previous chapter that defilement and slavery are merely the natural, inevitable consequences of our sin. Paul is saying here, 'Think again! God has actively given us over to them.' The expression 'give over' is courtroom language, as when the judge hands over the convicted criminal to the prison officer. It is a deliberate act on God's part. Does that seem unfair? Only if you think it is unfair of him to give us what we ask for. If we deliberately reject our maker's instructions, in the misguided belief that we know what to replace them with, is it any surprise that the maker is angry? He simply expresses that by handing us over to our desires, rather like a parent allowing a petulant son to eat as much chocolate as he wants, knowing it will make him sick. Its purpose is correction as well as just punishment, for God longs for people to turn back from their rebellion. As far as Paul is concerned, though, this is merely a foretaste of God's ultimate judgment. A day is coming when it really will be too late, when there will be no hope of correction.

In the future

> But because of your stubbornness and your unrepentant heart, you are storing up wrath against yourself for the day of God's wrath, when his righteous judgment will be revealed. God 'will give to each person according to what he has done' ... For God does not show favouritism ... This will take place on the day when God will judge men's secrets through Jesus Christ, as my gospel declares. (Romans 2:5–6, 11, 16)

One of the problems facing the Metropolitan Police when the first nailbomb went off in Brixton was that their hidden surveillance cameras were not working properly. If they had been, those killed in the Soho bomb would possibly still be alive today. Who can say? God is not like that. His surveillance is perfect – he knows everything about his world, he knows all the secrets of our lives. Furthermore, a day will come 'when God will judge men's secrets through Jesus Christ' (Romans 2:16). This is not a warning to ignore in the way that city-centre shoppers easily ignore the apparent crackpot wearing a sandwich board declaring that 'the end is nigh'. The day of judgment is a future certainty. It is as if, on that day, God will present a video of our lives, an accurate record of every word and deed, a video that even has subtitles to capture our every thought. After its première showing, he will give his verdict. When he judges 'each person according to what he has done', the essential criterion will be whether or not we have lived with God at the centre of our lives. As we have already seen, none of us can possibly claim an unqualified 'Yes'. The verdict is 'Guilty as charged'. Sure, we may not have planted nailbombs or swindled pensioners out of all their hard-earned savings, but we have all sinned. We have rejected God's rightful place in our lives, behaving as if he did not exist or could be safely ignored. The verdict is correct. The punishment is fair. Again, God gives us what we ask for. If we want existence without him at the centre, he gives it.

That is what hell is ultimately, for the experience of hell might be described as 'being cut off from God's benevolence and blessing'. It is the experience of being totally cut off from all the blessings and benefits that arise from a relationship with God. It is a truly terrible reality. In one place, Jesus represented it as 'the fiery furnace' (Matthew 13:42), and in another, as 'darkness' (Matthew 25:30); but in both references, he described the experience as one of 'weeping and gnashing of teeth' (Matthew 13:42). Elsewhere it is described as 'darkness', where there will also be 'weeping and gnashing of teeth' (Matthew 25:30). Why do you think Jesus used such grim imagery? Is he trying to scare people? The short answer is 'Yes'. That is precisely the point, because he longed for people to escape the horrors of hell. That, after all, was precisely what drove him to die on the cross, as we shall see. He never had the lurid fascination with hell that some medieval artists displayed; if anything, he downplayed its horror. His motive for mentioning it at all was pure love. If I spotted a fire in your house, I might have to scream to grab your attention to make you escape. You would quite probably be very scared, but that is immaterial. I would be doing the most loving thing I could do, as your fear would motivate your escape.

Of course, the question of hell raises many difficult issues, for which there is not sufficient space here.[11] The bottom line, though, is that God will be just. He will take into account our relative levels of knowledge and understanding. He will show absolute impartiality (Romans 2:11). We can be sure that he will not make any mistakes or give us any grounds for appeal. We will all recognize his justice, however grudgingly. Nevertheless, before we leave this subject, there are two questions we can briefly deal with here.

A world under judgment
Why the delay?
We, of course, live 2,000 years after Jesus. It is all very well to talk about this future judgment day, but after this length of time, it seems even more fanciful an idea now than it was in the first century. Nevertheless, there are grounds for considerable relief that the day has not come sooner. As Peter says: 'But do not forget this one thing, dear friends: With the Lord a day is like a thousand years, and a thousand years are like a day. The Lord is not slow in keeping his promise, as some understand slowness. He is patient with you, not wanting anyone to perish, but everyone to come to repentance' (2 Peter 3:8–9).

The fact that it has not happened before now should make us extremely grateful, not cynical. The delay is a mark of the kindness and mercy of God. This is not to imply that the delay will last indefinitely, since Peter knows that God 'is not slow in keeping his promise'. As Peter goes on to predict in his letter, sceptics will always scoff at the prospect of that judgment. The fact that there has been a 2,000-year delay only seems to give credence to today's scoffers. Do not believe them. Instead, be grateful for the delay.

What about us?
It should be clear from this whole chapter why judgment is good news. A world without judgment is hopeless and full of despair. It renders the crimes of the likes of Stalin, Hitler and Pol Pot meaningless, because they do not have to face any accountability

for their actions. Stalin, for instance, died in his sleep, immune to the demands of any human court. In contrast to worldly opinion, however, the Bible clearly states that God is in control of his world and that judgment will come, even for apparently invulnerable dictators. Our mistake is to think that we can draw a convenient circle on the ground around our feet and tell God to judge everyone outside it; but that is impossible. We stand guilty of sin, along with everyone else. The writer of Proverbs wrote centuries ago:

Acquitting the guilty and condemning the innocent –
   the LORD detests them both.
(Proverbs 17:15)

If that is the case, what hope do we have? Where can we turn?

When Napoleon was the emperor of France, a soldier in his army committed a crime that the emperor deemed worthy of execution. The soldier's mother came to him and pleaded with Napoleon to spare her son: 'Sire, please have mercy! Let him off this terrible punishment.' The emperor replied, 'Why? He doesn't deserve it.' The desperate woman retorted, 'Sire, if he deserved it, it wouldn't be mercy.' History does not relate what happened next, but the question remains for those of us who face God's perfect justice. Mercy is what we desperately need. Will we find it? The answer can of course be a resounding 'Yes!' The death of Jesus is our means to obtaining this mercy; so having laid out the very dark cloth on the counter, we can now proceed to examine the glories of God's sparkling diamond.

Summary

- Because God is absolutely pure and morally perfect in holiness, it is not possible for sinful human beings to approach him freely.
- Because he is holy, God must, in wrath, expose and condemn sin. However, in a world crying out for justice, we would not want it any other way.

Part 3. Messiah: God's gift

6. Messiah: the promise

Please read Isaiah 7:10–15; 9:1–7 and 53

Extending for over 4,000 miles, the Nile is the longest river in the world. It tends to be most closely associated with Egypt, but only a proportion of the entire river's length flows through it. One branch flows out of Lake Victoria and, before it leaves Ugandan territory, has already become a substantial river. It is at its most spectacular at Murchison Falls. After 15 miles of rapids, the river suddenly approaches a gap of only 15 feet through which an estimated 1,000 tons of water are propelled every second. It hardly seems possible for a torrent of this magnitude to fit through it. I have stood on the very edge of that gap, and been able to look down to the seething pools 120 feet below. It is both awe-inspiring and humbling to witness the power of such a huge river compressed into such a small area. No other natural watercourse on earth produces anything like this energy, and yet within only a few hundred feet of the falls, the river pans out again to resume its majestic course through Lake Albert to Sudan and Egypt.

Humanity's sin caused God a seemingly impossible dilemma,

but it was a dilemma he always knew how to solve. He knew how to show us mercy without undermining his holy justice. His perfect plan was to enter his world and deal with the problem once and for all. His was a radical plan and a uniquely simple plan. He would send his Son to die on a cross. This explains the book of Revelation's startling description of Jesus as 'the Lamb that was slain from the creation of the world' (Revelation 13:8). Incomprehensible though it seems, God always intended the cross. Just as the 15-feet-wide Murchison Falls is where the Nile's power is condensed, so is the cross the focus of God's wisdom and power. That he would invest so much in what appears to be such a tragic event is indeed initially bizarre, and yet those few hours that Jesus hung on the cross reveal more about the heart and character of God than any other event.

Hard though it is to grasp, God has revealed himself in the Bible as a Trinity. There are three members, Father, Son and Holy Spirit, who are all one, the one true God; and all three members of the Trinity were intimately involved in seeing the cross through. They played different roles, of course, but all were totally committed to it; the cross was to be the greatest and most gracious gift God would ever offer to his rebellious world. Our problem is that we rarely give it anything like the attention that it demands, which is extraordinary. How tragic that an event which is the primary subject of the praises of heaven is hardly valued by those who live on earth! A century ago, J. C. Ryle gave this vital warning, and it is as important today as it ever was: 'If you have not yet found out that Christ crucified is the foundation of the whole volume, you have read your Bible hitherto to very little profit. Your religion is a [sky] without a sun, an arch without a keystone, a compass without a needle, a clock without spring or weights, a lamp without oil ... Beware, I say again, of a religion without the cross.'[1]

The Spirit-revealed plan
We must start long before the arrival of Jesus on to the Palestine scene to understand why Ryle was right, since the Holy Spirit had

been at work for centuries preparing the way for his mission. The apostle Peter put it like this: 'the prophets ... searched intently and with the greatest care, trying to find out the time and circumstances to which the Spirit of Christ in them was pointing when he predicted the sufferings of Christ and the glories that would follow' (1 Peter 1:10–11).

Having studied a small part of Isaiah in the previous chapter, there is wisdom in staying with him to learn how Peter's assertion is worked out there. As we do so, we shall find that his confident statements about the future stretch our minds to breaking point. Isaiah himself must have been confused by some of them since, as they stand, they seem impossible to hold together. From the vantage point of living this side of the cross, however, we can see precisely what the Spirit was up to. The first example comes almost immediately after Isaiah's heavenly vision in chapter 6.

The birth of the God-Man
By this point in Isaiah's ministry, the king on David's throne in Jerusalem was Ahaz. He was therefore 'the messiah' of his day (since the word 'messiah' simply meant 'the anointed king of God'). The messiah had the responsibility for ruling God's people according to God's law for God's glory (as passages like Deuteronomy 17:18–20 make clear). Ahaz was certainly a shrewd political operator, as demonstrated by his opportunistic treaty with the Assyrian king (2 Kings 16; 2 Chronicles 28). His real problem, however, was that he had rejected a relationship with Israel's God, because he was more concerned about political power than spiritual faithfulness. He even sacrificed one of his own sons to a pagan god, which, in ancient Israelite eyes, was the epitome of pagan evil (2 Kings 16:3). Here Isaiah, speaking in God's name, records a conversation with the king:

> Again the LORD spoke to Ahaz, 'Ask the LORD your God for a sign, whether in the deepest depths or in the highest heights.'
> But Ahaz said, 'I will not ask; I will not put the LORD to the test.'

> Then Isaiah said, 'Hear now, you house of David! Is it not enough to try the patience of men? Will you try the patience of my God also? Therefore the Lord himself will give you a sign: The virgin will be with child and will give birth to a son, and will call him Immanuel. He will eat curds and honey when he knows enough to reject the wrong and choose the right.'
> (Isaiah 7:10–15)

Ahaz's reply gives the impression of being devout, but it was a sham. In a different context, his refusal to put God to the test would of course imply genuine piety, because testing God is expressly forbidden in the law (Deuteronomy 6:16). Jesus even pointed this out to his tempter in the wilderness (Matthew 4:7). Ahaz's problem is that God had explicitly told him to ask for a sign, 'whether in the deepest depths or in the highest heights' (Isaiah 7:11). Alec Motyer explains this as saying that God was prepared 'to move heaven and earth' to usher in this sign.[2] It would be very special indeed.

In the light of this, Ahaz's response was haughty, to say the least. It displayed rank unbelief, which explains Isaiah's reaction: 'Will you try the patience of my God . . . ?' The House of David, with its deeply flawed messiah, is now an infuriating failure. Its integrity and authority to rule over God's people are completely undermined. Worse still, its failure typified the moral failure of the whole people of Israel, bound as it was in sin and rebellion. Any suggestion that it could ever be God's means of solving human-ity's predicament was now laughable, because David's dynasty itself clearly shared humanity's problem. God's response to Ahaz's unbelief was consequently to say that he would start again. He would still send a sign, but instead of it being a product of trust, it would now condemn Ahaz and expose him as the compromised ruler that he was.

God's sign was to be no thunderbolt from heaven, nor a mass uprising from the fields of Israel. It was to be no less than the birth of a baby boy (verse 14). Royal births are always out of the ordinary, as journalists today know well; they tend to spark off great excitement. An insecure king might feel great anxiety, however, since new heirs can often grow up to be new threats. Still, public interest would be enormous. Isaiah predicted no ordinary royal birth, however. Notice the bizarre circumstances of the child's birth in verse 14. His mother was to be a virgin, and she would call him 'Immanuel'.

Sceptics have had a field day with this verse. For a start, it is said that the word for 'virgin' only means 'young girl', regardless of what sexual activity she has been involved in. It has been successfully argued, however, that this is not the case, and that Isaiah used 'the word which, among those available to him, came nearest to expressing "virgin birth" and which ... opens the door to such a meaning'.[3] Even if that seems implausible, it is his second detail that really stretches the mind, for 'Immanuel' actually means nothing less than 'God with us'. Again, a sceptic might say that this is a name born out of the piety of a mother who was perhaps grateful for God's help in the pregnancy and birth process. The boy's actual identity is not necessarily implied by his name at all. After all, there are many people with that name even today. When we come to Isaiah's prophecy two chapters later, however, such scepticism must be dispelled. What we find is hardly piety. It verges on blasphemy:

> For to us a child is born,
>> to us a son is given,
>> and the government will be on his shoulders.
> And he will be called
>> Wonderful Counsellor, Mighty God,
>> Everlasting Father, Prince of Peace.
> Of the increase of his government and peace
>> there will be no end.
> He will reign on David's throne
>> and over his kingdom,
> establishing and upholding it

with justice and righteousness
from that time on and for ever.
The zeal of the LORD Almighty will accomplish this.
(Isaiah 9:6–7)

To address any human being as 'Mighty God' or 'Everlasting Father' was blasphemy of the worst sort, for which the Old Testament had severe punishments.[4] Nevertheless, Isaiah predicted that this new Messiah on David's throne would be God himself and, despite a highly unusual conception, he would be born in the normal way.

How could that be possible? Isaiah is completely silent. He has no answers for us, presumably because he had none for himself. We are simply told that 'the zeal of the LORD' would bring it about (verse 7). He was God, after all; he can do it. He alone was able to cause a virginal conception. He alone was able to work out how to enter into the very world he created. This new Messiah would put Ahaz, and even David himself, in the shade, which means that there can be hope at last, says Isaiah. This was no pipe dream, because 'the zeal of the LORD will accomplish this'. No wonder this news brought great joy. As he says in the verses just before those quoted:

The people walking in darkness
    have seen a great light . . .
You have enlarged the nation
    and increased their joy . . .
    as people rejoice at the harvest.
(Isaiah 9:2–3)

With hindsight it is obvious whom this predicts: Jesus of Nazareth, the man who was God. Because of Isaiah's prophecies, we can see that he was no bolt from the blue. When John introduced his Gospel with 'The Word [who is God] became flesh and made his dwelling among us' (John 1:14), there should have been no surprises. The Old Testament made it perfectly clear that this would happen. Isaiah could never have conceived what it would be like to have a divine king walking the earth, nor does our retrospective knowledge of Jesus' life make it much easier for us to imagine it. The more we start trying to get our heads round Jesus' identity, the more we are stunned. It hardly seems possible that God should become human. To grasp its apparent absurdity, consider a situation whereby every dog in the world was in danger from some terrible disease. Imagine that the only way to help them escape was by your discarding your human nature, and becoming a dog. Then you'd be able to speak to them in a language they could understand and you could show them how to avoid the disease. The cost to do this would be great – you would have to leave behind your loved ones, your job, your hobbies, your interests. You would exchange them all for the world of the pet dog. It seems utterly ridiculous, and yet does it not capture something of what the Son of God did in becoming human? Does it not capture a hint of the sacrifice he was prepared to pay for our sakes?

The crucial point for our purposes is the consequence all this has for our understanding of the cross. As a result of becoming human, God was able to identify with us, his creatures. He got his hands dirty, as it were. As the writer of the letter to the Hebrews puts it: 'We do not have a high priest who is unable to sympathise with our weaknesses, but we have one who has been tempted in every way, just as we are ...' (Hebrews 4:15). He wept, he got tired, he was hungry, he felt the cold, he had fun, he mourned the deaths of friends, he was tempted to sin.[5] He was like us in every way – except one. Hebrews slips it in at the end of the verse just quoted: 'yet [he] was without sin'. In other words, he lived in perfect obedience to the Father in heaven. He resisted every temptation to go his own way, thus living in complete contrast to every other descendant of Adam. Combine this with his claims actually to be God, in fulfilment of Old Testament prophecy, and we end up with an explosive truth. Jesus is consequently able to be the perfect mediator between God and us.

Do you see why this is so important? When marriages break down, the only hope for reconciliation is often the intervention of a mediator, someone who is trusted by both parties to be fair. It is therefore important for both parties to sense that the mediator starts with some sympathy and understanding of each position; it may even help them to know that the mediator has experienced similar difficulties in his or her own life. This principle can be extended to God's relationship with humanity, a relationship that our sin ruined. Because Jesus is fully human, he can be a perfect representative *of* humanity. He knows at first hand what it is like to live as a human. He can plead our case to God. Because he is fully divine, he can be God's perfect representative *to* humanity. He can perfectly reveal the God to whom we must return. In the Old Testament, a temple priest acted as a mediator between God and us, able to enter parts of the temple forbidden for normal believers, but his ministry was always flawed by his own sinfulness. We shall return to this theme shortly, but because he is the divine man, Jesus is the great 'high priest'. He is the true mediator.

If this seems implausible, then there is yet another prophecy in Isaiah that will baffle us further. The New Testament leaves us in no doubt that it is to be closely associated with those of Isaiah 7 and 9. The Holy Spirit, through all three of Isaiah's prophecies, is pointing to one and the same man: Jesus of Nazareth.

The sacrifice of the God-Man

If you have not yet already done so, read through the whole of this passage from Isaiah. It is the fourth of four sections describing a mysterious Servant of God who will come to accomplish God's purposes, but it is easy to understand why he is not naturally associated with the baby born to David's throne. The Servant is both enigmatic and perplexing and, despite being described in the past tense, was still to emerge on to the world stage. Isaiah uses the past to convey the certainty of his future arrival.

A repulsive sight

When an accident happens on one side of a motorway, it is not uncommon for both sides to be snarled up by traffic. This is because cars on the opposite side slow down to get a glimpse of what has happened. People share a sinister fascination in tragedy. Get close enough to see what the victims actually suffered, however, and the healthy reaction is to look away. The sight is too grisly. It comes as quite a shock, then, to be told that God's Servant will cause a similar reaction:

> ... there were many who were appalled at him –
>> his appearance was so disfigured beyond that of any man
>> and his form marred beyond human likeness ...
> Like one from whom men hide their faces
>> he was despised, and we esteemed him not.
> (Isaiah 52:14; 53:3)

The Servant's pain and agonies were such that it was impossible to look for long. The sight repelled even the most sympathetic onlookers. The question demanding to be answered is, 'Why does he suffer like this?'

A deliberate sacrifice

Isaiah's prophecy is dominated by the extraordinary and initially unpalatable idea that this was all God's deliberate plan:

> ... yet we considered him stricken by God,
>> smitten by him and afflicted.
> ... the LORD laid on him the iniquity of us all ...
>
> Yet it was the LORD's will to crush him and cause him to suffer ...
> (Isaiah 53:4, 6, 10)

That seems obscene. What conceivable purpose could God have for doing this? We can fully grasp this only if we have the

Old Testament sacrificial system in our minds. In the Jerusalem temple God had provided a temporary means to deal with sin. The idea was that you took an animal to the temple to be sacrificed as a means of shielding you from the consequences of your sins. The animal would symbolically take the punishment you deserved. It acted as a substitute. As the mediator between you and God, the temple priest would perform the sacrifice for you, and the result was that your sin would be forgiven. However, the whole system was never designed to be more than an elaborate but potent illustration. As the writer of Hebrews says, 'it is impossible for the blood of bulls and goats to take away sins' (Hebrews 10:4). An animal could never be a perfect substitute for a human being.

Think of the national football squad. We are familiar with the idea of 'X playing for England' or 'Y for Scotland', and so on. The players represent their country and if the tabloid Press trust the manager's decisions, most people are happy to let them be their representatives. Imagine that one of them is injured during a big match. A substitute needs to be brought on to replace the incapacitated player and so enable the team to resume at full strength. It would not do to use someone who had no experience of playing for the team, which is why someone else from the bench is brought on. When that happens, not only is that new player a representative of his country; he is also a substitute for the injured player.

If we extend the analogy to our fallen world, we are faced with the uncomfortable reality that there is no-one left on the field – it is as if sin has incapacitated every member of the human race. There is no-one capable of representing us and acting as our perfect substitute. Our predicament requires a radical solution. God's plan, therefore, was to send his Servant to act both as our representative and as our sacrificial substitute, to enable us to be freed from the burden of sin. Notice in this verse how Isaiah, to emphasize this point, builds up the contrast between the Servant and those for whom he substitutes:

But *he* was pierced for *our* transgressions,
    he was crushed for *our* iniquities;
the punishment that brought *us* peace was upon *him*,
    and by *his* wounds *we* are healed.
(Isaiah 53:5; my emphasis)

We have already established that God must judge and punish our sin. Here, we find that his Servant has taken that punishment on himself. Let us be clear what the Bible is teaching here. This is not simply a situation whereby Jesus somehow removes the guilt of a particular sin, as if it were all very vague. Thinking like that avoids the need to allude to God's being angry; but however unpalatable that thought is, we cannot escape the fact that God *is* wrathful. Consequently we must understand Jesus' death as the means by which that wrath is diverted (what theologians call *propitiation*). A common illustration for this is a lightning conductor. Electric storms can seriously damage electrical items in a house, and so a copper rod is used to draw the lightning bolt away from the house's interior and earth it safely. Similarly, Jesus died on the cross to divert on to himself what we deserve. Like all illustrations, however, this has its limits because it cannot convey the personal aspects of propitiation. Sin is offensive to God and his holy anger demands justice, as we have already seen. Propitiation enables this anger to be transferred to the substitute, so that he experiences its full force instead. God's anger is then satisfied and spent, and the sinner can be forgiven.

At first sight, this is altogether objectionable and barbaric. Some have even described it as 'cosmic child-abuse', wherein the Father is inflicting the most appalling torment on his victimized Son. Where is the justice in that? It seems completely unacceptable. After all, where is the difference between this and the violence of ancient pagan rituals? Take the following particularly gruesome practice, for example:

> If Spanish chroniclers can be believed, the Aztecs sacrificed 20,000 to 50,000 people a year in their capital, Tenochtitlan ... To feed the

need for such huge numbers of victims, the Aztecs arranged a peculiar agreement with their neighbours to fight regular ceremonial battles not for conquest, but to allow each side to capture large quantities of sacrificial victims. Apparently most of the victims seized in what was called the War of Flowers considered sacrifice an honour or an unquestionable act of fate.[6]

In order to make the Aztec gods favourable, they needed to be brought round by the gruesome bribes of human lives. Worse still, there could never be any certainty that their prayers would be answered, so more sacrifices were constantly required to bolster their claims. We find that repulsive, and rightly so.

There are vitally important differences between this and what Isaiah predicted. The key lies in the Servant's identity and the one on whose initiative his sacrifice was made. Once we combine the three prophecies of our study, it starts to make sense. For, as we have said, the Servant of Isaiah 53 is none other than the Messiah of Isaiah 7 and 9. The Servant is no innocent third party, unjustly and barbarically dragged in to intervene in the breakdown in human–divine relations. No! He is the royal God-Man, come into the world to bring God's light into sin-caused darkness. He alone combines the nature of God and humanity. He alone can intervene on God's behalf to act as humanity's representative and substitute. He alone is untainted by sin and guilt, to the extent that he can take the full effects of God's punishment for others' sin on himself. As the great Bible commentator C. E. B. Cranfield brilliantly put it, 'God ... purposed to direct against his own very self in the person of his Son the full weight of that righteous wrath which [humanity] deserved.'[7] This is God's idea: it is an idea embraced by, and carried out by, each member of the Trinitarian Godhead, which means that it is an idea fully embraced by Jesus himself. To use Paul's words, 'God was in Christ reconciling the world to himself' (2 Corinthians 5:19). It is God's initiative and gift to humanity. And he did it because he loves us. That is not cosmic child-abuse! That is awesome, breathtaking love, a love that was prepared to pay the highest price for the sake of people who deserved nothing from him. To suggest otherwise is an unfortunate misreading at best.

The sixteenth-century German Reformer, Martin Luther, would read out Bible passages at meal times for his family devotions. One day, he read the account of God testing Abraham's faith by asking him to offer Isaac on the altar (in Genesis 22). Before he reached the point where a ram was substituted in Isaac's place at the last minute, his wife Katie shouted out, 'I can't believe it; God would never treat his own son like that!' 'But Katie,' Martin replied, 'he did!' God sent his Son to die on the cross in order to be our propitiatory sacrifice. He died, taking upon himself 'the punishment that brought us peace' (Isaiah 53:5).

Some object to the concept of Jesus needing to die for us like this. They say they could never believe in a God who expects that sort of sacrifice to be made. What this reveals, however, is not so much a reasonable and liberal understanding of God, as a complete underestimation of both the seriousness of our sin and the anger it provokes in a holy God. If we understood this, we would not argue with Isaiah's (and indeed the whole New Testament's) explanation of the cross. Instead, we would be on our knees in profound gratitude and relief, for, on the cross, our great high priest also became our great and unique sacrifice.

Summary

- God had always planned to send a Messiah who would be the ultimate bridge between himself and humanity – the God-Man.
- The cross was always intended to be central to the Messiah's mission, as the ultimate means of dealing with sin.

7. Messiah: the execution

Please read Mark 15

British newspapers were dominated by one news item on Thursday 7 February 1952. This was the account in *The Times*:

> It was announced from Sandringham at 10.45 a.m. to-day, February 6th 1952, that the King, who retired to rest last night in his usual health, passed peacefully away in his sleep early this morning.[1]

For centuries, the death of a British monarch has had major political implications. Sixteenth-century England, for example, was thrown into decades of turmoil by the death of Henry VIII. George VI's death hardly had that significance, and yet it still had repercussions. *The Times* continued:

> The Duke of Edinburgh broke the news to the new Queen in Kenya. After hurried preparations had been made, they flew from their little landing ground near Nyeri to Entebbe, Uganda, to join their airliner *Atalanta* [for the return to London] ... The Accession

Council, at a brief meeting at 5 p.m. yesterday, signed the
Proclamation of Queen Elizabeth II ... The sittings of Parliament
were suspended after members had been informed of the King's
death. Both Houses met again later for members to take the oath
of allegiance to the new Sovereign.

The King is dead! Long live the Queen! The death of any
monarch is inevitable. Some die violently, others in their sleep;
but all still die, for all are human. Every death is tragic. George VI
had been suffering from cancer for some time, and his death
naturally caused great sadness. Nevertheless, we would never say
that it achieved anything. Instead, death brings an end to life's
achievements. The king's death had consequences, of course, but
we would never call them achievements.

The contrast with the death of God's king could not have been
more marked. Yes, the Messiah died, and yes, it had consequences.
The surprise is that it was also his finest achievement! For it was
precisely through his act of dying that Jesus achieved his victorious
rescue.

Jerusalem-bound

Those who met Jesus were astonished by his powers. They had
never seen or heard of anyone like him. His ability to teach and
hold an audience put the so-called 'teachers of the law' to shame.
He could drive out demonic powers with a simple command
(Mark 1:21–26); he could cure someone's leprosy with a simple
touch (Mark 1:40–45); he could heal someone's chronic illness
with a simple word (Mark 2:1–12). Not surprisingly, he gained
quite a reputation: 'The people were all so amazed that they asked
each other, "What is this? A new teaching – and with authority!
He even gives orders to evil spirits and they obey him." ' News
about him spread quickly over the whole region of Galilee' (Mark
1:27–28). His authority and healing powers by themselves were
magnetizing; couple them with Jesus' wonderful character, and he
was irresistible. This is how one preacher described him:

Here was a man who exemplified supreme unselfishness but never self-pity; humility but not weakness; joy but never at another's expense; kindness but not indulgence. He was a man in whom even his enemies could find no fault, and where friends who knew him well said he was without sin. Surely no one could suggest that a man with a character like that was evil or unbalanced?[2]

Just imagine all the good he could achieve for the world. Think of the university theology faculties that could do with a decent lecturer, or churches that could do with a decent preacher! Think of the hospitals that could employ him as their combined Infectious Diseases and Orthopaedic Consultant. Think of the model of profound integrity he could have brought with him into public life and politics. Instead, he threw it all away. While still only in his early thirties, he deliberately threw it all away. For at the heart of his mission was neither an exorcism ministry nor a healing ministry – he came to die. And preaching was important because through it he could make that purpose clear. Using his favourite title for himself, Jesus declared, 'even the Son of Man did not come to be served, but to serve, and to give his life as a ransom for many' (Mark 10:45). Astonishingly, his death was the greatest contribution he could ever make to human society; which was why he was determined to go through with it, despite all the objections of those who loved him the most. His ministry was therefore dominated by his journey to Jerusalem, because that was where he would die. 'As the time approached for him to be taken up to heaven, Jesus resolutely set out for Jerusalem' (Luke 9:51). The next ten chapters in Luke's account are peppered with brief references to Jerusalem, constantly reminding us of the impending fulfilment of Jesus' mission.

Jesus was not acting on his own, but was obeying his Father's will. We can see this most clearly in his agonized night in the Garden of Gethsemane. Overwhelmed by the prospect of his imminent death, he prayed, 'Father ... everything is possible for you. Take this cup from me. Yet not what I will, but what you will' (Mark 14:36). Furthermore, the Holy Spirit was at work throughout his ministry, driving him on to fulfil the prophecies that he had been preparing for centuries. This is symbolized by the Spirit's startling involvement at the start of Jesus' public ministry: 'And the Spirit immediately drove him out into the wilderness. He was in the wilderness for forty days, tempted by Satan' (Mark 1:12–13, NRSV). This marked the spiritual battle Jesus faced throughout his ministry, which culminated in the cross. The Spirit was constantly at work keeping him on track. So what did the cross actually mean for Jesus? To answer that we come to Mark's account of the crucifixion itself.

Midday blackout

Eclipse-mania gripped millions all around the world on 11 August 1999. While it provoked ludicrous extremes of hysteria among some, there is no doubt that a full solar eclipse is a remarkable phenomenon. For a few minutes, at points along a certain trajectory, there is complete darkness, accompanied by an eerie silence, as birds and animals fall silent in their confusion. Even at our home in Sheffield, which experienced only a partial eclipse, the effects were astonishing, if brief. We felt an unmistakable drop in temperature. Once it was all over, however, life carried on as normal. For those who had heeded the advice not to stare directly into the eclipse, nothing significant changed. The moment of wonder passed.

Mark describes a similar event in his Gospel, but this one changed the world. This was no mere natural phenomenon, since it was designed to have profound significance. He is a brilliant storyteller, but he is much more besides. He packs his racy and compact narrative with momentous details. Because he has obviously left a great deal out, what he does say is all the more important. No word is wasted.

At the sixth hour darkness came over the whole land until the ninth hour. And at the ninth hour Jesus cried out in a loud voice, *'Eloi,*

Eloi, lama sabachthani?' – which means, 'My God, my God, why have you forsaken me?'

When some of those standing near heard this, they said, 'Listen, he's calling Elijah.'

One man ran, filled a sponge with wine vinegar, put it on a stick, and offered it to Jesus to drink. 'Now leave him alone. Let's see if Elijah comes to take him down,' he said.

(Mark 15:33–36)

Jesus' last words to be recorded by Mark are certainly strange. They confused the onlookers, who not unreasonably thought that he was calling Elijah. Elijah was one of the great prophets of the Old Testament, whose return had been prophesied by Malachi (Malachi 4:5). This was not what dominated Jesus' tortured mind after those hours hanging on the cross, however. He was in fact quoting from another Old Testament passage: the first line of Psalm 22. There is a simple reason for that: it was the closest scriptural description of what he was experiencing. He quotes it precisely because he *was* forsaken by God. Jesus, the Son of God, was cut off from his Father in heaven, for, as was noted in chapter 2, 'anyone who is hung on a tree is under God's curse' (Deuteronomy 21:23).

To ensure we grasp the correct interpretation, Mark drives his point home by describing the darkness. In the Old Testament, darkness during the day was symbolic of God's judgment. The classic example was the ninth plague on Egypt, described as 'darkness that can be felt' (Exodus 10:21). The prophet Amos announced impending judgment on Israel in these terms: 'I will make the sun go down at noon and darken the earth in broad daylight' (Amos 8:9). The point is clear. As Jesus hung there on that cross, he was not merely experiencing the punishment of a rigged human court; he was being judged by his Father. He did not deserve punishment from either, and yet he willingly bore the transfer of guilt from the guilty to the innocent, from sinners to the sinless one, from us to him. This marked Jesus' most complete identification with sinful people. We shall never fathom how this could have happened, but the signs are clear. The events fit perfectly with the interpretation given elsewhere in the Bible. Why else would Jesus cry out in forsakenness? Why else would darkness come over the earth as he hung dying?

This means that we must be careful in describing Jesus' agony. It is not unusual to hear people refer to his physical pain. That was undoubtedly terrible, since a cross was possibly the most horrific instrument of torture ever devised. The process of dying would be extended over hours if not days. Jesus' emotional pain was also appalling. He faced the torment of betrayal and loneliness, as all but a handful of his closest companions deserted him in terror. Nevertheless, these were nothing compared to his spiritual agony. We shall always tend to underestimate that because we can have little conception of the intimacy of his relationship with his Father. He endured fatherlessness for our sake. To put it more starkly, he went to hell for us. Incomprehensible though this is, Jesus went 'where God is not'. If ejection from the presence of God is what we deserve for our rejection of God, then this is what Jesus took on himself. This was the consequence of his substitution for sinners. If this interpretation seems questionable, then the apostle Paul soon removes any doubt. In fact, he presses the boundaries of our understanding even further: 'God made him who had no sin *to be sin* for us – so that in him we might become the righteousness of God' (2 Corinthians 5:21; my emphasis). An exchange has occurred. Jesus takes on my sin, and I am offered his right-eousness, his moral perfection that enabled him to relate to his Father perfectly. He took the punishment I deserved, which is why his substitution is technically called *a penal substitution* ('penal' meaning 'punishment-related').

The cross therefore proves how seriously God takes sin. Sin must be judged, even if it is borne by Jesus himself. It also proves how committed God is to saving sinners, for it was the Father who sent him there. Because of the substitution, the Father looked down on the crucified Jesus and did not see the perfect Son who always obeyed and loved him. Instead he saw the worst swindler, molester, rapist, corrupt official, criminal, liar, murderer, materialist – above all, the worst rebel the world has ever known. So he judged him for it.

There is mystery here, and an air of awed silence and reflection is perhaps the only worthy response initially. It is a unique event, not comparable with anything else in human experience. Thus no illustration taken from life can ever hope to communicate its profundity and complexity. In particular, it is impossible to find any parallel to convey the penal aspect of Jesus' substitution. Nevertheless, what drove Jesus to endure willingly the punishment that we deserved? It was love – his love for us. And we *can* find parallels to reflect that. In fact, Louis de Bernières deliberately evokes Jesus' substitutionary love in his bestseller *Captain Corelli's Mandolin*. Here is his account of his protagonists' executions by Nazi soldiers after the Italian forces joined the Allies towards the end of the war. It is worth quoting a couple of paragraphs:

> The carnage had none of the ritual formality of such occasions that film and paintings might suggest. The victims were not lined up against the wall. They were not blindfolded, faced away, or faced forward. Many of them were left on their knees, praying, weeping or pleading ... Some stood smoking, casually as at a party, and Carlo stood to attention next to Corelli, glad to die at last, and resolved with all his heart to die a soldier's death ...
>
> [After the shooting began, the soldiers], wheeling and dancing in the horizontal rain, were crying out. They fell to their knees, their hands flailing, their nostrils haunted by the stench of cordite, searing cloth and oil, their mouths filling with the dry and dusty tang of blood. Some stood up again, holding out their arms like Christ, baring their chests in the hope of a quicker death, a shorter route through pain. What no one had seen ... was that at the order to fire, Carlo had stepped smartly sideways like a soldier forming ranks. Antonio Corelli, in a haze of nostalgia and forgetfulness, had found in front of him the titanic bulk of Carlo Guercio, had found

his wrists gripped painfully in those mighty fists, had found himself unable to move ... Carlo stood unbroken as one bullet after another burrowed like white-hot parasitic knives into the muscle of his chest ... [Eventually Carlo] flung himself over backwards. Corelli lay beneath him, paralysed by his weight, drenched utterly in his blood, stupefied by an act of love so incomprehensible and ineffable, so filled with divine madness, that he did not hear the sergeant's voice.[3]

The fundamental weakness in this illustration is that in no sense can it be used to reflect the punishment Jesus endured for us. It is offensive in the extreme even to suggest that the action of the Nazi firing squad is in any way analogous to the Father's role at Calvary. Nevertheless, that last description is stunning: 'an act of love so incomprehensible and ineffable, so filled with divine madness'. De Bernières deliberately created in Carlo's death a stunning echo of the cross. Like Carlo, Jesus' supreme motivation for going to the cross was not duty or obligation; it was incomprehensible love, except that, for Jesus (in full and willing partnership with the Father), it went far wider than love for one man. Their love burned for the whole of humanity.

We cannot leave the story there, however, since Mark has more to tell.

Divine access

With a loud cry, Jesus breathed his last.

The curtain of the temple was torn in two from top to bottom. And when the centurion, who stood there in front of Jesus, heard his cry and saw how he died, he said, 'Surely this man was the Son of God!'

(Mark 15:37–39)

Mark would have made an excellent video editor! He knows the power of placing apparently random details side by side to tell his story. We're with him watching the heart-breaking events on Golgotha Hill outside Jerusalem, only to find ourselves suddenly whisked away to the Temple Mount at the heart of the city. Before we can catch our breath, though, we are returned to hear the astonished words of a Roman soldier. These 'fast-edits' all help to explain what was happening at the point of Jesus' death.

The temple dominated the Jerusalem skyline, but it was an ambiguous symbol. On the one hand it symbolized the ancient Jewish confidence that God dwelt at the heart of his people, since the temple existed to sustain their relationship with him. From the earliest points in their history, God had promised, 'I will be with you' (Exodus 3:12). The temple thus stood for the restoration of the friendship with God first lost in the Garden of Eden. On the other hand, the temple acted as a monumental 'No Entry' sign. Using the Eden imagery again, it acted as the flaming sword at the gate of Eden, barring humanity's entry into God's presence (Genesis 3:24). Because of human sin, public entry into the presence of the holy God is both prohibited and impossible. There could only be one exception: the Old Testament stipulates that only one man (the high priest) on only one day a year (the Day of Atonement) could enter the temple's inner sanctum (the Holy of Holies). He could do this only after going through elaborate purification rituals.

The Holy of Holies was separated from the rest of the building by a huge curtain or barrier (see diagram on p. 95). It was this curtain that Mark describes being torn in two as Jesus died. The implication is that access is no longer the preserve of one man on the Day of Atonement, and that full atonement is now available to all who wish to receive it. What precisely does that mean?

Think back to Isaiah's vision in the temple (Isaiah 6). Coming into the presence of God brought him face to face with his own sin, as we saw in chapter 5 of this book. The story did not end there, however, for a strange incident followed. 'Then one of the seraphs flew to me with a live coal in his hand, which he had taken with tongs from the altar. With it he touched my mouth and said,

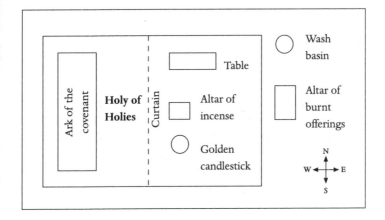

"See, this has touched your lips; your guilt is taken away and your sin atoned for" ' (Isaiah 6:6–7).

Isaiah was safe in the presence of God in his vision. His protection came from the live coal removed from the altar. Its significance lies in the fact that the altar was where the blood from the substitutionary sacrifices was poured, thus diverting God's wrath on to the sacrifice. The believer could then be freed from his or her guilt. In the words of the seraph, 'guilt is taken away' and 'sin atoned for'. The word 'atoned' literally means 'covered'. 'Just as we speak of a sum of money as sufficient to "cover" a debt, so [atonement] is the payment of whatever divine justice sees as sufficient to cover the sinner's debt, the death of the substitute sacrifice on the altar.'[4]

Once atonement has been achieved, access into God's presence in absolute safety is available. The way to remember it is to say that if we have atonement, we have at-one-ment with God – we are covered and are therefore safe.

On the cross the ultimate price was paid, the ultimate sacrifice was offered. Jesus, the God-Man, the great High Priest, made atonement for all who would come to him. As a result, the barrier to God was torn open. The No Entry sign was removed, and access to the top is now available to all. The barrier that had lasted ever since Adam and Eve's expulsion from Eden was demolished. Note that the curtain was torn down from 'top to bottom' (Mark 15:38). This was God's initiative and God's achievement; it was something humanity could never have pulled off. Mark's dramatic fast-edit visit to the temple gives us a glimpse of how God did it: through Jesus' provision of *substitutionary atonement*. With his death, the temple was now obsolete. No longer was a symbol of God's presence required, because God had been among his people in Jesus. No longer was a symbol of God's impenetrable holiness required, because God had provided the ultimate sacrifice of atonement in Jesus. A priesthood is no longer necessary, for the great High Priest has provided the ultimate mediation. Everyone, regardless of religious or racial background, can now have access to the top through Jesus. It is no accident, then, that the first person to acknowledge Jesus' identity as he died was a pagan soldier, who exclaimed, 'Surely this man was the Son of God' (Mark 15:39). That statement forms the climax of the whole of the Gospel. At the cross, the soldier confessed precisely what Mark wanted his readers to confess.

Summary

Mark's account is compact. It is left to the rest of the New Testament to flesh out the meanings and implications of this extraordinary event. Peter, in common with every other New Testament writer, draws on Old Testament ideas to explain it, and brilliantly compresses it into one memorable phrase: 'Christ died for sins once for all, the righteous for the unrighteous, to bring you to God' (1 Peter 3:18). If we break that down into its constituent parts (see diagram on p. 97), we can see clearly why it summarizes everything we have been thinking about.

It is important to keep reminding ourselves whose initiative all this was. God took on himself, in his Son, the full force of the judgment that we deserved. As a result, rebellious human beings like you and me can experience the joys of being true children of God, as we shall go on to explore. Jesus was no innocent, unjustly

1 Peter 3:18	The interpretation of the cross	
Christ died	= *the event*	***Jesus' sacrifice** to provide a:*
for sins once for all	= *the need*	**penal** *sacrifice*
the righteous for the unrighteous	= *the process*	**substitutionary** *sacrifice*
to bring you to God	= *the effect*	**atonement** *sacrifice*

punished third party. He is God himself. The cross is therefore a victory of 'divine self-satisfaction through divine self-substitution'.[5] It was what Jesus was determined to endure. It was what the Spirit was determined to prepare for and lead Jesus to fulfil. It was what the Father was determined to achieve. And they all did it out of love. This is what the King and Lord of all creation is like, and those are the lengths to which he is prepared to go.[6]

8. Messiah: the blood

Theatrical blood seems to be a regular feature of modern life. The average number of shootings we witness each year on screens small or large is often calculated, although, as far as I know, the amount of blood we see has not. It must add up to at least several gallons a month! Yet, whatever the amount, we still know it is not genuine. Even if we are temporarily swept up in the drama of *ER* or *Prime Suspect*, most of us have the capacity to switch off and get up to make the tea! It is a different story when it comes to real blood. The sight of it can make even the least squeamish blanch. Some panic, while others look away. So it is no wonder that the squeamish can find the Bible difficult, for the blood of Jesus is a major biblical theme. Someone has calculated that it is referred to at least forty-three times in the New Testament. It is even something that Jesus discussed at his final meal with his friends. With only hours to live, he instituted a very strange means to commemorate his death. As they went through the centuries-old Passover ritual, Jesus suddenly inserted new and startling words into the script. As he handed the wine cup round, he said, 'Drink from it, all of you. This is my blood ... which is poured out for many for the forgiveness of sins' (Matthew 26:27–28). With words like that, is it any wonder that one of the most common ancient misconceptions about Christians was that they were cannibals? Jesus' symbolism is truly gruesome. Taken out of context, it is bizarre, to say the least. Placed within the framework of the whole Bible, however, what he says is fundamental to understanding his death.

Blood in the Bible

In a world that obviously knew nothing of the medical advances of the twentieth century, the sight of blood was especially serious. Heavy bleeding was immediately life-threatening, and unless it could be stopped, death was inevitable. Heart-pumped blood sustains life. As the Old Testament law puts it, 'the life of every creature is its blood' (Leviticus 17:14). Once shed, life slips away. In the Bible, however, its connotations are even more sinister. This is how one biblical commentator sums it up: 'the Hebrews understood "blood" habitually in the sense of "violent death" (much as we do when we speak of "shedding of blood").' [1]

The violent connotations of blood have even fuller biblical significance when put into the context of the very event Jesus was celebrating on that fateful night, the Passover.

The exodus story has recently recaptured the public imagination thanks to Hollywood's blockbusting *The Prince of Egypt*. The film is particularly effective in its account of the Passover. After a battle between Yahweh, the God of Israel, and Pharaoh, the stubborn 'divine' king of Egypt, Yahweh eventually sends the ultimate judgment on Egypt. Every firstborn male, whether human or animal, Jewish or Egyptian, is to die. Yahweh thus proves his ascendancy over all rivals. Pharaoh's father had attempted something similar when he first ordered the murder of all Jewish male infants, but his orders were never fully carried out (Exodus 1:16, 22). Yet, when Yahweh judges, he is always impartial. He cannot simply ignore the Israelites. They are no less sinful than the Egyptians. The difference is that he provides protection for those who turn to him.

Each household is to sacrifice an unblemished lamb or a goat, and then, before roasting it for supper, they have to smear their front doorframe with the animal's blood.

> 'On that same night I will pass through Egypt and strike down every firstborn – both men and animals – and I will bring judgment on all the gods of Egypt. I am the LORD. The blood will be a sign for you on the houses where you are; and when I see the blood, I will pass over you. No destructive plague will touch you when I strike Egypt.'
>
> (Exodus 12:12–13)

Blood on the doorframe indicates both to the household's inhabitants and to Yahweh that a death has occurred there. An animal has died to protect the life of the firstborn son. It is a substitution: one death instead of another's. The Israelites are thus made safe from God's judgment, not because they do not deserve judgment, but because God in his mercy has provided a substitute – the Passover lamb. That fateful night arguably had more impact on the life of Israel than any other.

Jesus' symbolism at his final Passover celebration becomes clearer in the light of this. By modifying the ancient ritual he did not simply provide an updated version; he was instead identifying his own mission with that of the lamb killed in each home centuries before. His own death was by implication to be a substitute for those who would follow him. That is what his blood symbolizes. Whenever the theme of his blood recurs in the New Testament we are always to understand by it his substituting death: his death instead of mine. In one sense, this merely repeats what has been said in the previous chapter, but it is essential to understand the significance of his blood if we are to grasp the wonder of what Jesus did. According to the New Testament, everything flows from his substitutionary death. Penal substitution is not, as some suggest, one illustrative model among many, from which we can choose what we like best. It is the *primary model* on which all the others depend. This becomes apparent when we study the effect of Christ's blood. What follows is by no means an exhaustive list, since Jesus' accomplishments on the cross are far too awesome to be restricted in that way. Nor are the consequences mutually exclusive; there is inevitably overlap. Taking these four, however, does indicate how perfectly Jesus' substitutionary death dealt with our predicament.

Justification

To be pronounced guilty by a judge in a court of law cannot be a pleasant experience. It must be particularly uncomfortable if there is a time lag between the verdict's announcement and the sentencing. One's imagination about what is to come must run riot. Of course justice must be done and be seen to be done, but can there be no room for leniency? It is a legitimate question. When it comes to our standing before God, is the question not even more legitimate? Surely he longs for a restoration of his relationship with us? But what about our guilt? While we may hope for leniency when it comes to God's judgment of us, we are unable to deny our guilt.

This is a problem we too easily underestimate. Many Christians today rightly focus on the need for our relationship with God to be restored after our alienation from him brought on by sin. Too often, however, that alienation is made to eclipse our guilt as the most serious problem. One reason for this is simply that the need for reconciliation with God is a more palatable image than the need for guilt to be forgiven. Yet the plain reality is that there can be no reconciliation without guilt being first dealt with. At the heart of this lies the idea of justification.

The apostle Paul thought a great deal about justification. The theme crops up in many of his letters, but it is most dominant in Galatians and Romans. In the latter, he wrote these startling words: 'Since we have now been justified by his blood, how much more shall we be saved from God's wrath through him!' (Romans 5:9).

The point is that because of Jesus' death in our place, we can be 'justified'. In other words, we can be made right with God. We shall all face the judgment of God at the end of our lives, but to be justified is to have advance notice of the verdict. We can know with certainty that we shall be acquitted or declared 'not guilty'. It is a legal term with relational implications. Our judge and enemy can become our forgiving friend. Justification is not the same as reconciliation, though they are interrelated: justification frees us from our guilt, which thus opens the way for reconciliation.

Charles Simeon was a Cambridge minister at the end of the eighteenth century. When he arrived as an undergraduate in Cambridge in 1779, he understood little of the Christian message. A note requiring his attendance at a college Communion service three weeks later filled him with horror. He wrote, 'Satan himself was as fit to attend as I,' and immediately went out to buy some books explaining Communion. He spent three months trying to make sense of it. A particular mystery to him was what relevance the cross could have to his sense of guilt, but there was no-one on hand to whom he could turn. Then he suddenly came upon this phrase: 'The Jews knew what they did when they transferred their sin to the head of another.' In a flash, it came to him: 'I can transfer all my guilt to another. I will not bear it on my soul one moment longer.' He later wrote:

> Accordingly, I sought to lay my sins upon the head of Christ. On the Wednesday, I had a hope of mercy. On the Thursday that hope grew. On the Friday and Saturday, it became more strong. And on the Sunday morning, Easter Day, April 4th, I woke with these words on my lips: 'Jesus Christ is risen today. Halleluia! Halleluia!' From that hour peace flowed in rich abundance into my soul, and at the Lord's Table in our chapel I had the sweetest access to God, through my Saviour.[2]

Our guilt is transferred to our substitute, Jesus Christ. That is why he suffered so much on the cross. He was taking on himself the punishment our guilt deserves. That is what it means to be 'justified by his blood'. As Paul sums it up, 'Therefore, there is now no condemnation for those who are in Christ Jesus' (Romans 8:1). Through the cross, our guilt has been dealt with once and for all. Once we have been justified, we can then be reconciled to God. What Simeon discovered in Easter 1779 is still the case today.

The threat of fire on the North American Prairies is very real. Once a farmer and his daughter were out walking across some of their vast farmland. In the distance, they spotted a prairie fire. Because the wind was driving the fire towards them, they knew they had only one chance for survival. They quickly lit a fire where they were and ensured that it burned a large patch of grass around them. When the flames of the larger fire approached, they stood on their burnt patch. The child was terrified, but her father assured her, 'the flames can't get us. Fire can't burn the same place twice.' The confidence that Christ offers is similar. Because of the punishment he has taken for us, we can be sure that justice has both been done and seen to be done. The fire of God's wrath will not strike twice in the same place. He took what I deserved for my guilt so that I can be declared not guilty: 'We have now been justified by his blood.'

Another illustration of this comes from the story of William Callahan. He was a homeless criminal until he came to trust Jesus Christ for himself at a Christian meeting. He tried to live down his pre-conversion reputation, but found it hard. The police kept him under constant surveillance, refusing to believe that someone like him could be reformed. After five years of this he went to Chicago and, through the aid of a Christian lawyer, retrieved his photos from the police. He did not want to be known as a crook any longer. Then he tried the prison authorities. The reply from them was curt: 'You may have got the records from the police, but you can't get them away from the State of Illinois.'

Some years later, in ill health, he found himself giving a testimony of his conversion at a meeting attended by no fewer than three state governors (including the Governor of Illinois, John

Atgeld). By the end Atgeld was wiping tears from his eyes, and said to Callahan, 'I'll see what I can do.' A month later William received a letter from the governor. 'My dear Mr Callahan, it gives me pleasure to enclose your photo from the Penitentiary of Joliet, and to tell you that your records there have all been destroyed. There is no record, except in your memory, that you were ever there. You have the gratitude and best wishes of your friend, John P. Atgeld.'[3]

While this story may seem legally implausible these days, it perfectly illustrates what it means to be justified. Through what Jesus did, the records of our sin have been destroyed. It is as if God even forgets about them. As the writer of the psalm sang:

> He will not always accuse,
>   nor will he harbour his anger for ever;
> he does not treat us as our sins deserve
>   or repay us according to our iniquities.
> For as high as the heavens are above the earth,
>   so great is his love for those who fear him;
> as far as the east is from the west,
>   so far has he removed our transgressions from us.
> (Psalm 103:9–12)

In dying, Jesus has done everything that needs to be done; he has suffered every punishment that needs to be suffered. No matter how terrible the individual acts of rebellion we have committed, he has dealt with the guilt. We shall return to the theme of justification in a later chapter.

Reconciliation

We have seen already, however, that our sin and guilt are deeply personal. It is not that we have disobeyed rules *per se*, but that we have lived without God at the centre of our lives. In other words, our relationship was broken off. Jesus' death on the cross is our means to its restoration. The restoration of any broken human relationship, whether in a struggling marriage or between nations at war, will always be tough and costly. It will require forgiveness, usually from all sides. As C. S. Lewis once noted, 'Every one says forgiveness is a lovely idea, until they have something to forgive.'[4] Forgiveness is costly but essential if there is to be any hope for reconciliation.

We must be careful here. It is not possible to draw an exact parallel from human relationships to our relationship with God. Two significant differences need clarification. First, there is no need for mutual forgiveness. God has done nothing that requires forgiveness. We are the ones in the wrong, not him. Secondly, there is the place of the cross itself. Why does Jesus have to die? Why doesn't God 'just forgive'? After all, when human beings forgive each other, we would never dream of demanding a sacrificial death. That would seem to miss the whole point! So why does God demand one? If anything, it makes him seem *sub*human. We forget, however, what we have just considered. Our rejection of him is not merely hurtful to him; it is also culpable. We have rebelled against our rightful ruler, we are guilty and justice must be done. We are all prone totally to underestimate the seriousness of our predicament. We require not just forgiveness, but also the aversion of God's holy anger. That is why he can't 'just forgive us'. As one writer said, 'forgiveness is to man the plainest of duties; to God it is the profoundest of problems'.[5]

Once we have grasped these differences we can begin to appreciate the wonderful forgiveness available through Jesus' death. With forgiveness in a broken relationship there can be reconciliation. This is how Paul puts it: '[God was pleased through Jesus] to reconcile to himself all things ... by making peace through his blood, shed on the cross' (Colossians 1:20).

The tragedy of the fall has been reversed. A rebellious world is able to return to submit to its rightful Creator and Lord, all because that Creator and Lord shed his blood. Humanity had been alienated from God since the fall, barred from his presence by the sword flashing across the entrance to the Garden of Eden (Genesis

3:24). The temple curtain has been torn open (Mark 15:37–38) so that we can be reconciled to our Creator – because *he* unilaterally took the initiative to reconcile us.

As the new century opens, the West finds itself amid great uncertainty. Western Europe can claim to have enjoyed peace for over fifty years – no mean feat considering the previous fifty – but it is not 'peace' as the Bible understands the word. After all, not far beyond the EU's borders the Balkans are riven with conflict. Then there is the Middle East with its apparently intractable problems. Within the EU itself national interests constantly cause wrangles and angry exchanges, not to mention the tragedies of Northern Ireland and the Basque region of Spain. Yet we still call it 'peace'. What we mean by the word, therefore, is merely the absence of overt, conventional warfare, whether there are conflicts on other levels or not. Zhou Enlai was, for a number of years, Prime Minister of the People's Republic of China. He was surely not far off the truth in his chilling remark that 'All diplomacy is a continuation of war by other means.'[6] While extreme, perhaps, he at least faces up to the harsh realities of politics around the globe. So much, then, for peace.

When God reconciles humanity to himself, bringing peace, he means it. It is not merely the absence of war. It means at the very least the full restoration of friendship. Paul, in another place, links it with the justification we have just been considering: 'Therefore, since we have been justified through faith, we have peace with God through our Lord Jesus Christ' (Romans 5:1). We now have nothing to fear when we come into God's presence, in total contrast to the Israelites who gathered at the foot of Mount Sinai for the giving of the law. They were petrified (see Exodus 19:18–19 and Hebrews 9:18–21). We are reconciled; we have peace. Hostilities have ceased.

The implications of this do not stop there. If there can be peace with God, there can also be peace within humanity, and the rest of creation. If sin caused alienation at every level, Jesus' death can bring reconciliation at every level. This is crucial. Western

Christians are often accused (with good cause) of focusing too much on the personal and individualistic implications of Christ's death. Christ's reconciling work, however, has public, corporate and even global scope. God's purpose was not a private trans-action for me alone, as if I were the centre of the world, but rather a plan for the restoration of *all* creation. Accepting God's reconciliation, therefore, forces me to open my eyes to everyone and everything else in his creation.

Antoine Rutayisire is a remarkable Christian minister working in and around some of Rwanda's prisons. They are overcrowded places, full of those who were involved in the terrible genocide of the mid-1990s. Despite his belonging to the minority, but previ-ously powerful, Tutsi tribe, Antoine is desperately concerned to see reconciliation between Hutus and his own tribe. Decades of mutual hostility have left their marks. In fact, Antoine's father was killed by Hutus, and he himself was sacked from his lecturing post simply because of his tribe. He has now concluded, however, that the only hope for tribal reconciliation is for people to be reconciled to God first. In a recent interview, he had this to say: 'Spiritual healing is Rwanda's greatest need. They say we should build houses and provide saucepans and blankets, and leave the deeper issues until later. But when the genocide happened, did we not have houses, saucepans and blankets? This is not a problem of saucepans and blankets – it is a problem of hearts.'

This is no ivory-towered theorizing. It is born out of his own experience. He went on to describe how his dismissal from the university was the last straw: 'I was very angry, and I had a long list of people I hated – with just cause. But it was during that time that I met the Lord Jesus.'

Soon after this, much to his own astonishment, he found himself praying these words: ' "God, do you really mean to tell me that I can love even the people who killed my father?" ' He then prayed for help to forgive each name on his list. 'When I had finished that exercise, 20 years of hatred and bitterness were wiped out in one day.'[7]

How else could someone find himself working among the very tribe he had every reason to hate? This is the testimony of a man who knows what it means to be reconciled to God, who knows how much his sin alienated him from God. It is also the testimony of someone who fully appreciates the incentive a forgiven sinner has to forgive others. Peace with God must and does lead to peace with others – a point Paul makes explicitly after the following quotation from Ephesians. The foundation stone on which God creates his new people, the church, is the reconciliation between Jews and Gentiles. Up until that point, the ethnic chasm between them was unbridgeable. 'His purpose was to create in himself one new man out of the two [Jew and Gentile], thus making peace, and in this one body to reconcile both of them to God through the cross, by which he put to death their hostility' (Ephesians 2:15–16).

If as great a division as that between Jews and Gentiles can be overcome, then what is to stop every other split being overcome? We should expect nothing less in people who have been brought into peace with their Creator God. The real tragedy is that all too often Christians don't work these implications through into their own lives. Depressingly, this seems to have been the case among many Christians in Rwanda itself, some of whom were actually implicated in the genocide.

Finally, because of our reconciliation to God, we can and should be reconciled to the rest of creation. Who could fail to be concerned at the way we human beings have often needlessly exploited God's creation? Evidence for the extent of the damage we have inflicted on it is overwhelming. Yet it is all the inevitable outworking of humanity's alienation from it after the fall. Being reconciled to God must give us renewed concern to be the good creation-stewards we were created to be. We may disagree about the best priorities and methods; and we must avoid the New Age trap of heading into nature-worship or Gaia-worship. Christians worship the Creator, not his creation. That we are to be stewards of God's earth, however, we cannot deny.

Hope for reconciliation between peoples and individuals, and between humanity and the created order, can ultimately be found only in God. When people are reconciled to him through the shed blood of Jesus, lives are changed for ever. We are restored to the relationships that we were created to have. Thus the effects of the fall begin to be reversed. This helps to explain the urgency of the ministry Paul (in common with all Christians) was called to, which has at its centre the plea to be reconciled to God. As he says to the Corinthian Christians: '[God] reconciled us to himself through Christ and gave us the ministry of reconciliation: that God was reconciling the world to himself in Christ, not counting men's sins against them. And he has committed to us the message of reconciliation' (2 Corinthians 5:18–19).

Redemption

In December 1997, a woman made redundant by a London borough council was awarded £234,000 for sexual discrimination. Esther McLaughlin's award was then a record pay-out, though it has no doubt been eclipsed since. The two years at the council had been a terrible ordeal for her: 'I was made to feel that I had no contribution to make and that I was basically worthless. I felt isolated. It was like being bullied and I lost my confidence. A year before, I had achieved an MBA. They picked on me simply because I was not part of the long-established male network of directors.'[8]

That is a dismal indictment of her former employers, yet she is by no means unique. Workplace bullying is sadly a common phenomenon, despite the prevailing assumption that people's indulgence in bullying was left behind in the school playground. It is striking, though, how Esther McLaughlin's sense of worth was affected. Her experience faces us with potentially unnerving questions. Why did she feel the way she did? Where in fact should we find our sense of worth?

Tough calculations are being made about other people's worth every day, whether cynically or with heavy hearts. Company directors must do this as they plan for the future, with the constant risk of treating employees as mere resources or even economic liabilities. What is the value of keeping someone employed, and who should pay for it? Military leaders face similar issues. How do you value the life of one man caught behind enemy lines? What is a price worth paying? This is the emotive issue at the heart of Stephen Spielberg's successful film about the Normandy landings, *Saving Private Ryan*. A squad of American GIs is sent into enemy territory to rescue Private Ryan after all three of his older brothers have been killed. It is a mission that costs the lives of nearly all the rescuers, but the mission is nevertheless a success. The impossible question hangs over the film: was it worth it?

For most of the time, however, it is the sense of *our own* worth that concerns us most. We are constantly trying to gauge it from a variety of factors – our roles and jobs, our experiences, our family background. Above all, most would agree that a sense of worth (or lack of it) is derived from our relationships. So it comes as no surprise that Esther McLaughlin felt the way she did.

What few people acknowledge is that the Creator of the universe has put a value on each human being that far exceeds anything the world has to offer. This is how the apostle Peter describes what has happened to a Christian: 'For you know that it was not with perishable things such as silver or gold that you were redeemed from the empty way of life handed down to you from your forefathers, but with the precious blood of Christ, a lamb without blemish or defect' (1 Peter 1:18–19). Paul says something similar: 'In him [Jesus] we have redemption through his blood, the forgiveness of sins' (Ephesians 1:7). That is how much God values his human creatures. For him, the shed blood of his Son was a price worth paying. That is the extent of his love, and at its heart is this idea of redemption. To understand it we must return to the exodus.

The Israelites had been enslaved in Egypt for generations. By the time of Moses' birth, conditions had deteriorated significantly, and the people cried out to God for help. After all, he had promised to make the descendants of Abraham, Isaac and Jacob into a nation with their own territory. In Egypt, the promises must have seemed hollow. God did eventually come to their rescue, however. Before it all happened, he explained what he was going to do: 'I am the LORD, and I will bring you out from under the yoke of the Egyptians. I will free you from being slaves to them, and I will redeem you with an outstretched arm and with mighty acts of judgment' (Exodus 6:6).

The rescue was going to be spectacular. After the dramatic events of the Passover, God would lead the Israelites miraculously through the parted Red Sea (Exodus 13 – 14). Pharaoh would be powerless to prevent their departure. The people would be free. This great liberation would always lie at the heart of what the Old Testament understood by redemption.

Redemption would have had another connotation for the original readers of the New Testament: the world of the slave auction. It is an alien world to us, full of injustice and horrific cruelty, but it was a fact of life two millennia ago. A slave was a person's property and a price needed to be paid for his or her life – a ransom, if you like. Imagine a slave-owner visiting the auction. Suppose he has become a Christian since selling off his former slaves. When he realizes that their conditions have significantly deteriorated, he decides to buy them back for the express purpose of improving their lot. That 'buying back' of what was originally his is redemption.

We can now begin to see how Christ's death redeems us. Our redemption cost him his blood, his life. In fact, Jesus even described it as a ransom himself (Mark 10:45). He does not aim to buy back old slaves for his own sake, for he has nothing but our best interests at heart. He wants to liberate us, and that liberation is what lies at the heart of redemption. Having bought us back, however, there is a sense in which we now belong to him. The paradox is that to be owned by Jesus is truly liberating. As he himself said, 'if the Son sets you free, you will be free indeed' (John 8:36). This was the way we were created to live: according to the Maker's instructions. It is the freedom of the fish that would rather thrive in the confines of a pond than be given the chance to 'enjoy' the freedom of the open air. Being free to live for and be owned by Jesus is the natural environment for which we were created.

Like all analogies, we must not push the biblical idea of redemption too far. In contrast to what some medieval Christians thought, Jesus did not have to pay some cosmic auctioneer to free us. Nor are we to imagine that God sold us off in the first place – we have already seen how we are responsible for our own desertion from him. We are meant to hold to the redemption analogy only in so far as it illustrates that the price for our freedom was his blood.

Slavery to Pharaoh is not our problem these days. As we know, we are enslaved to something far more sinister – our sin. Through what Jesus did on the cross we can be rescued from sin's dominating power. Its grip is then loosened and it will one day be completely removed. How this works out we shall consider in chapter 10. For now, it is enough to say that our situation is no longer hopeless. God's character and his law, which are the expression of his perfection, are no longer a threat to those who know they can never live up to them. Because of Jesus' death, however, it is now possible to live for God, as part of his family. This is how Paul sums it up: 'we were in slavery under the basic principles of the world. But when the time had fully come, God sent his Son, born of a woman, born under law, to redeem those under law, that we might receive the full rights of sons . . . So you are no longer a slave, but a son; and since you are a son, God has made you also an heir' (Galatians 4:3–5, 7).

Daughters could not inherit property in the ancient world, which is why, in his letter to the Galatians, Paul deliberately describes Christians of both sexes as equally 'sons of God' (Galatians 3:26–28). He is making a profound point in the quoted verses: both men *and* women can become sons of God through the redemption Christ offers. This means that we can all equally inherit the treasures of his kingdom. We can all be adopted as members of God's family, regardless of our gender, social status, or nationality: 'There is neither Jew nor Greek, slave nor free, male nor female, for you are all one in Christ Jesus' (Galatians 3:28). To be redeemed by Christ means the incredible privilege of being adopted into his family. From slaves, we can become sons. This is precisely the point Jesus made just before the verse quoted above: 'Now a slave has no permanent place in the family, but a son belongs to it for ever. So if the Son sets you free, you will be free indeed' (John 8:35–36).

An orphan once lived in a large house with his ageing grandmother. In the early hours one night, the house tragically caught fire, and in her attempts to rescue her grandson, the old woman died. He was then trapped. The boy's cries for help were eventually answered by someone who climbed an iron drainpipe to rescue him. Some days later, a public hearing was held to decide who should receive custody of the boy. A farmer, a teacher and the town's wealthiest citizen all put forward their claims. Throughout, the boy resolutely stared at the ground.

Then a stranger walked to the front and slowly removed his gloves to reveal the terrible scars on his hands. The crowd gasped, but the boy shouted out in recognition. He saw that they were the hands scarred by the searingly hot drainpipe during his rescue. It was no surprise to anyone there that this man, and not the others, was deemed to have credentials appropriate for adopting the boy – scarred hands. Now, Jesus offers a far greater rescue, though he also bears scars on his hands to prove it. He bought our rescue with his life. That is a price tag to top every other, yet it is a price God is willing to pay to redeem us. This stamps each human being with a value greater than we could ever imagine in our wildest dreams. Worth like that will not necessarily remove the insecurities that Esther McLaughlin suffered immediately; but it would certainly provide the secure foundation from which to begin to combat them.

Cleansing

Blood leaves one of the hardest stains to remove from clothes. Living in the era of Daz and Ariel Automatic, we forget that, as we assume that it is not difficult to make our whites 'whiter than white'. In an age that knew little if anything of detergents, however, blood could mark the end of a cherished garment. This fact alone would have made John's vision in Revelation even more startling for its original readers than it is for us:

> Then one of the elders asked me, 'These in white robes – who are they, and where did they come from?'
>
> I answered, 'Sir, you know.'
>
> And he said, 'These are they who have come out of the great tribulation; they have washed their robes and made them white in the blood of the Lamb.'
>
> (Revelation 7:13–14)

It is a bizarre image, though, in the context of everything said so far, it makes perfect sense. The blood of Jesus, far from defiling or polluting those who come into contact with it, has the opposite effect. It cleanses. It purifies. Above all, it removes whatever prevents a person's entry into the presence of a holy God. So here is yet another angle on what the substitutionary death of Jesus achieved. We can be cleansed by the sacrifice of the Lamb.

The writer of the letter to the Hebrews uses the same imagery:

> The blood of goats and bulls and the ashes of a heifer sprinkled on those who are ceremonially unclean sanctify them so that they are outwardly clean. How much more, then, will the blood of Christ, who through the eternal Spirit offered himself unblemished to God, cleanse our consciences from acts that lead to death, so that we may serve the living God!
>
> (Hebrews 9:13–14)

The difference between Jesus' blood and that of other sacrificial victims is that Jesus deals with the heart. He goes much deeper than external, ritual cleansing. He deals with the conscience, an essential requirement if defiled sinners are to be able to return to God. This is what anyone who cannot ignore the skeletons in their cupboard longs for. The cross is in fact their only hope. It does not matter what those skeletons are. The blood of Jesus is powerful enough to remove any and every trace completely; and that includes any who have on their consciences deeds as extreme as those of Lady Macbeth (described in chapter 4). That is why everyone who puts their trust in what Jesus achieved on the cross can be confident that the day will come when they will be made cleaner than they could ever dream possible. That is the wonderful inheritance that Jesus promised we will enjoy at his return.

We have already acknowledged that all these effects of the cross are interlinked, so it should come as no surprise that our cleansing is closely related to our justification. When we put all four together we can perhaps begin to understand why there is something offensive about them: they force us to recognize yet again the utter helplessness brought by our sin. There is nothing that we can contribute to our rescue. If the only way for us to be justified, reconciled, redeemed and cleansed was for Jesus to die as our substitute, our predicament must be very serious indeed.

The story is told of George Bernard Shaw storming out of a meeting where the cross was being explained in terms similar to those we have been considering. He left shouting, 'I'll pay my own debts!' He went on to write about what he described as 'crosstianity',[9] which he saw as an aberration of pure Christianity. A religion that has a Messiah who needs to die on an instrument of torture, punished in our place, was something to be utterly despised. He saw it as undermining a religion of forgiveness, which he regarded as the heart of genuine Christianity.

Of course, he failed to grapple with what we have already discussed in this chapter. It is surely not hard to detect wounded pride at the heart of his objections, which would explain why Shaw wanted nothing to do with the cross; but surely wounded pride is a small price to pay for the confidence Jesus' death can bring? David Gooding puts it brilliantly: 'Some people's sense of values is strange. Religion that urges them to moral behaviour but never gives them any sense of complete acceptance with God – that they value highly. Salvation, which can give them forgiveness and complete acceptance with God now, and certain hope for the future – that they not only reject: they despise it.'[10]

That is what the finished work of Christ is all about: having complete assurance of the new status and new future that comes through Jesus. Because he died, I know I am safe.

Mary desperately needed a blood transfusion. The doctor explained to her brother, Johnny, that as he had recovered from the same disease, her only chance for survival came from a transfusion of Johnny's blood. 'Would you give your blood to Mary?' the doctor asked. The boy's lower lip started to tremble. Then he smiled, and said, 'Of course.' Soon the children were taken into the hospital room – Mary, pale and thin; Johnny, strong and healthy. Neither spoke, but when their eyes met, Johnny grinned. Then the nurse started taking his blood, and towards the end of his ordeal, Johnny tremblingly asked, 'Doctor, when do I die?' Only then did the Doctor realize why there had been any hesitation in Johnny's mind. And still he had gone ahead with it.[11]

Our problem requires a solution far more serious than a simple medical procedure. Nothing less was required than the Son of God giving his blood for us, but for him it really did mean giving up his life. That voluntary shedding of his blood is awe-inspiring. That is true love, the wonder of the cross.

Summary

Let us draw these thoughts together with those of chapter 4 like this:

Sin's effects		The victory of the cross	Because Christ died as our substitute
We are guilty		*Justification*	We have now been *justified* by his *blood* (Rom. 5:9)
We are alienated	HIS DEATH	*Reconciliation*	[God was pleased through Jesus] to *reconcile* to himself all things ... by making peace through his *blood*, shed on the cross (Col. 1:20)
We are enslaved		*Redemption*	In him we have *redemption* through his *blood* (Eph. 1:7)
We are defiled		*Cleansing*	The *blood of Christ* ... [will] *cleanse* our consciences from acts that lead to death (Heb. 9:14)

9. Messiah: the triumph

Official records claim that General John Sedgwick was killed in action in the Battle of the Wilderness during the American Civil War. Sadly, the truth is not so straightforward or valiant. As he was inspecting the troops, he came to a parapet that faced enemy lines, whereupon his officers discreetly suggested that he duck while passing. 'Nonsense,' the general is reputed to have snapped. 'They couldn't hit an elephant at this dist–'[1]

The expression 'famous last words' could have been invented for General Sedgwick! In everyday language, the phrase describes statements we are bound to regret. We will rue the day we ever said them. This is not to say that a person's last words are always embarrassing or to be regretted. They can sometimes actually express a sense of regret. Regardless of what one might think of his exploits, Cecil Rhodes, as noted in chapter 3, achieved an incredible amount for one man. The end of his life, however, was marked by a severely damaged reputation after personal scandals and the Boer War (for which he was largely responsible). As he lay dying of heart disease, his friend Lewis Michell heard his final murmurings, 'So little done, so much to do.'[2]

The contrast with Jesus could not be greater. During his agonized last hours he found the energy to speak a number of times. We have already considered his cry of forsakenness, and we will go on in the next chapter to look at his words to the thief executed beside him. Before he commended himself to God (Luke 23:46), however, he spoke again: 'Later, knowing that all was now completed, and so that the Scripture would be fulfilled, Jesus said, "I am thirsty." A jar of wine vinegar was there, so they soaked a sponge in it, put the sponge on a stalk of the hyssop plant, and lifted it to Jesus' lips. When he had received the drink, Jesus said, "It is finished." With that, he bowed his head and gave up his spirit' (John 19:28–30).

Those last three words – 'It is finished' – contain the grounds for all Christian confidence, and summarize everything that makes the Christian message unique.

Our debt discharged

'It is finished' could sound like a cry of resignation and despair, like the words of a man who has lost his final chance to save his own life. That is not the sense of it at all. The English translation obscures John's vital point, because he in fact repeats one word three times. The same Greek root-word (*teleō*) is translated in verse 28 by 'completed' and 'fulfilled', and in verse 30 by 'finished'. Each is a legitimate translation, because the word carries all three nuances. The accumulated impact of John's repetition, however, is that it shows that Jesus' cry of 'It is finished' was no cry of defeat or regret. Far from it! It was a cry of victory. It meant that what the Old Testament anticipated, Jesus was fulfilling. For example, he called out for a drink in verse 28, to fulfil Psalm 69:21. He then cried out, 'It is finished,' because he knew that his agonized mission was completed, his work accomplished. Execution on a cross does not give the appearance of victory, but as we know, appearances were deceptive. This is brought home when we appreciate a fourth nuance that *teleō* has. If you pay in advance for an item on order from a shop, you may well be given an invoice rubber-stamped with the date and the word 'Paid'. You then have no obligation to pay anything else, and the shop is bound to give you the item as soon as it comes in. Jesus' victory cry can similarly be translated 'Paid!' The point is obvious. What we deserve to pay as punishment for our sin, he has paid for us. With his death on the cross our debt is discharged – it does not need to be paid twice.

Not only does this rubber-stamp all the implications of the cross considered in the previous chapter; it also points us to a wonderful reality about God. As Jesus breathed his last, he offered the astounding confidence that we cannot be loved any more than we are by God; nor can we be loved any less. What greater commitment to us could Jesus show than by dying for us? This is the wonder of what is called grace. Grace has been correctly defined as 'God's undeserved mercy', but that makes it seem bland. God's grace is his provision for us, his enemies, of every-thing required to restore us to friendship with him. We are guilty and deserve punishment. Instead, God forgives and acquits. That is truly mind-blowing! That is grace! That is the heart of the gospel, the Christian good news, and that is what marks it out as unique.

Our situation is like that of an Internet shopping addict who clocks up hours and hours online, surfing everything from Amazon to eBay. To make matters worse, he manages to get hold of other people's credit card details and accumulate huge bills on other accounts. Eventually he is caught, and charged with fraud. The bills on his victims' accounts are then transferred to his own, making him bankrupt. The debt is too great for him to deal with himself. He is helpless. The debt caused by our sin is similarly overwhelming; and yet Jesus' offer to all who follow him is that his death pays our debt of sin for us. He does for us what we could never do for ourselves.

Many people view God as a demanding God. In fact, all religions other than Christianity picture God like this in some way, so that he constantly expects us to do more for him. Only Christianity tells of a God who is more ready to give than we are to ask, a God who takes the initiative before we even realize initiatives need taking.

That takes us to the heart of the character of God. The cross keeps forcing us to refocus our concept of God. Do we imagine him constantly wagging a reproachful finger at us? Is he constantly demanding that we strive to be better, do more, live perfectly? Does this leave us in despair or deep anxiety? The cross must dispel these images for good, since it proves that God knows our weakness and frailty all too well. Why else would Jesus have gone to die for us there? The Christian God anticipates our inability to keep his standards by taking the consequences of our failure on himself. What other religion or belief system can claim to have a God who shows such generosity, such self-sacrifice, such grace?

His decisive defeat

Waterloo has become a byword for great victories in British military circles. The battle there marked the termination of Napoleon's hopes for European control, to the extent that a colloquial expression to describe someone's downfall is that he or she 'met their Waterloo'. England in the first few hours after the battle had a very different perspective, however. In the days before telegrams, a semaphore system was the only means of communicating news speedily over large distances. The message would be signalled from lookout to lookout, until it eventually reached London and beyond. When the first ship with news crossed the English Channel, it started signalling to the lookout on the top of Winchester Cathedral. The first word came: 'Wellington'. Then the second: 'defeated'. At this point the elements seemed to play a cruel trick: fog suddenly descended, and the message stopped. Gloom descended over all those who heard the news, since they then feared the worst. Within a couple of hours, however, the fog lifted, and the signal could continue: 'Wellington defeated the enemy!'

For those followers who watched or heard about Jesus' death, the news must have been bleak. Their inevitable gloom must have driven them to assume the worst: 'Jesus defeated.' The reality could not have been more different. Within forty-eight hours, people were being brought face to face with the true victor of the cross, and it was neither Pilate nor Caiaphas, but the risen Jesus. He had defeated the enemy. He had come back to life. He had won. It was not enough for Jesus simply to destroy the terrible consequences of sin. For his mission to be completely fulfilled he needed to destroy sin's causes as well. We must therefore grapple with what Jesus was really up against.

Satan defeated

There is no mystery about who Jesus' opponents were on the surface: the Roman and Jewish authorities. It was they who formed an unholy alliance to have him eliminated. It was they whom Jesus defeated through his apparent defeat on the cross: 'having disarmed the powers and authorities, he [Jesus] made a public spectacle of them, triumphing over them by the cross' (Colossians 2:15).

Common Roman military practice was to parade defeated enemies in what was called a 'triumph'. Displaying all the booty plundered from the conquered land, the generals would lead representatives of the newly enslaved nation through the streets of Rome, all for the delight of the huge city crowds. Yet again the invincible might of Rome was proved. Using this imagery, Paul claims in this verse that Jesus' death on the cross was itself a 'triumph'. Do you see the wonderful irony there? Tom Wright puts it like this: 'These powers, angry at his challenge to their sovereignty, stripped *him* naked, held *him* up to public contempt, and celebrated a triumph over *him* ... [Paul] declares that, on the contrary, on the cross God was stripping *them* naked, was holding *them* up to public contempt, and leading *them* in his own triumphal procession – in Christ, the crucified Messiah.'[3]

To suggest that Jesus' crucifixion was itself a 'triumph' must have sounded absurd, and yet when he cried, 'It is finished,' Jesus overcame all the world's attempts at asserting its control over

God. When he was raised from the dead, God vindicated the way of the cross as the way to serve him and not the way of imperial or religious power.

The Roman and Jewish alliance cannot be understood in isolation, however. It is obvious from the rest of the Bible who lay behind them. Genesis 3 had introduced the existence of a power-hungry enemy who is desperate to exploit every opportunity to destroy or spoil whatever God does. Satan is a merciless bully, who 'prowls around like a roaring lion looking for someone to devour' (1 Peter 5:8). Consequently, he was determined to destroy Jesus' mission. That is why Satan orchestrated the world's implacable opposition to Jesus. So when Paul speaks of Jesus' triumph, it is not just the Roman and Jewish powers who were defeated; Satan was defeated as well. Notice how Jesus described his impending death in these terms, referring to Satan as 'the prince of this world': 'Now is the time for judgment on this world; now the prince of this world will be driven out. But I, when I am lifted up from the earth, will draw all men to myself' (John 12:31–32). With his death and resurrection ('lifted up' refers to both), Jesus proved that the battle had been won: Satan is a defeated enemy.

Some will object to this, not because they necessarily find it hard to believe in the existence of Satan, but because they cannot believe that he really has been defeated. How can the horrors of Auschwitz and Belsen, for example, be described as anything but satanic? The suffering and tragedies that dominate our world did not cease 2,000 years ago. So where is the evidence for this great victory? Why has the world not improved? An explanatory illustration can be found in the events of another military victory, though this one is more recent. The Allied landings in Normandy towards the end of the Second World War led to swift conquests on the European mainland. After D-Day, the Nazi forces were driven back with remarkable speed. With the Soviet victories in the East, Hitler's fate was sealed. The decisive battles had been won, but the war was by no means over. There was still further bloodshed and heavy conflict to come, and the world had to wait almost a whole year after D-Day for Germany's surrender and VE Day.

Satan's downfall is similar. His decisive and unequivocal defeat was achieved at the cross. His demise is guaranteed. The day will come when he will be 'thrown into the lake of burning sulphur', to quote the book of Revelation (Revelation 20:10). In the meantime, however, he strives and struggles, refusing to accept the inevitable and determined to cause as much damage as he can. His eventual demise will coincide with Jesus' return and judgment of the world. The reason it is delayed is to provide the opportunity for all to turn to Jesus, as we saw at the end of chapter 5. As we wait for that day, we must take God's word for it about Satan's end. Just as the full experience of being justified will not be felt until that day, so must we wait patiently for the repercussions of Satan's downfall. Then we shall see Jesus' victory in all its glory. As we wait, however, we can take advantage of the firstfruits of this victory. 'Satan' means 'adversary or 'accuser'.[4] It is a fitting name because he loves to accuse us of our guilt long after the cross has wiped it away. He will persist in his attempts to make us believe that we are still unfit for God's presence. He will do everything he can to distract us from the confidence of our forgiveness that the cross provides.

Satan's supreme weapon is deception, which is why the New Testament also calls him the 'father of lies' (John 8:44). When Jesus cried, 'It is finished,' he meant it. He cannot be contradicted. Our confidence in Satan's ultimate exposure and defeat is found at the cross, as the book of Revelation puts it:

> For the accuser of our brothers,
>   who accuses them before our God day and night,
>   has been hurled down.
> They overcame him
>   by the blood of the Lamb
>   and by the word of their testimony . . .
> (Revelation 12:10–11)

Satan's guaranteed demise has one final implication that we have overlooked: we can trust that our last enemy will also be conquered. The writer of Hebrews described Satan as the 'one who holds the power of death' (Hebrews 2:14). With his decisive defeat, death is no longer the threat it once was.

Death defeated

When the evidence for Jesus' resurrection was first put to me I began to take his claims seriously, for it had never previously occurred to me that it was anything more than a fairy tale. If the resurrection is something you have never investigated for yourself, I strongly urge you to begin such an investigation.[5] There can be little doubt that crucifixion killed Jesus, as that is one of the best-attested facts in ancient history. The issue is, what happened to his body after he died? Two quotations will suffice here to whet appetites for those who wish to pursue this.

Commenting on the fact that Jesus' dead body was never displayed by anyone (including the Roman and Jewish authorities), Ravi Zacharias makes this vital observation:

> There is something often missed here. If the disciples were fabricators of an ideal, they could have merely posited a spiritual resurrection, which could have been done even with the presence of a dead body. Instead, they went the hard way, by talking of the resurrection of the actual physical body, which, if not true, was an enormous risk should the body ever have been detected. No, they believed in a literal resurrection because they had witnessed it.[6]

No wonder the preaching of the first Christians was filled with such zeal and conviction. For not only was Jesus' resurrection incredibly exciting; it was also fundamental to their belief. If the resurrection did not happen, then Christianity was entirely false. As Paul said, 'if Christ has not been raised, your faith is futile; you are still in your sins' (1 Corinthians 15:17). It did happen, however, which explains the very existence of a church at all. This is what a

Jewish scholar, Pinchas Lapide, has to say about the claims for Jesus' return to life:

> How was it possible that his disciples, who by no means excelled in intelligence, eloquence or strength of faith, were able to begin their victorious march of conversion ...? ... In a purely logical analysis, the resurrection of Jesus is 'the lesser of two evils' for all those who seek a rational explanation for the worldwide consequences of that Easter faith ... Thus, according to my opinion, the resurrection belongs to the category of the truly real ... A fact which indeed is withheld from objective science, photography and a conceptual proof, but not from the believing scrutiny of history ...[7]

It is not enough for Jesus simply to have returned to life. If I ran out on to the main road near my home and was knocked down by the Number 60 bus, I hope I would be missed. If I came back to life a few days later, people would no doubt be astounded and also, I hope, pleased! But that would not make me divine. God may well have been involved, and there would be all kinds of explanatory theories, but few (if any) people would spontaneously think I was God incarnate!

Why was it any different with Jesus? The clue comes from the events preceding our respective resurrections. Suppose that before my accident, I had made specific claims about my identity and future. If I had predicted that I would rise again, everything would then be very different. My resurrection would suddenly take on supreme importance: it would vindicate any other claims that I had made, however preposterous they might first have appeared. That is precisely what happened with Jesus. On a number of occasions he specifically predicted that his death would be followed by a return to life. See, for instance, Mark 8:31; 9:32; 10:33–34. When it actually came true all his other claims about himself were thoroughly vindicated. Everything he was seeking to achieve through his death would be endorsed. His mission would truly be *seen* to be 'finished' when he beat death at its own game by rising back to life.

Human death had never been part of God's original design for people made in his image. Jesus' resurrection changed everything. Death has at last been overcome; it no longer has the last word, and life is no longer as meaningless as it sometimes feels. Jesus has been the trailblazer, breaking a way through the ultimate barrier for all time. To grasp precisely what that means, we must distinguish resurrection from resuscitation. It is possible for someone to be at death's door, and even be deemed dead according to certain medical criteria, but then breathe again. That is resuscitation, because death will still come again. It is as if the person has entered the tunnel of death only to re-emerge through its entrance (Figure A). The time will inevitably come, however, when they will re-enter it, as death is still the 'dead end' that it always was (Figure B). That was true for all the people whom Jesus raised from physical death during his lifetime, including Lazarus in John 11 and Jairus's daughter in Mark 5.

Jesus' resurrection was fundamentally different: he broke through the tunnel, never to die again. By emerging from the other end he achieved what no-one before or since has ever achieved (Figure C).

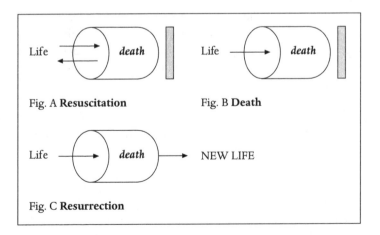

Fig. A **Resuscitation**

Fig. B **Death**

Fig. C **Resurrection**

Jesus' resurrection therefore overcame the final consequence of sin. Paul ties this to the Christian believer in startling ways. He states that those who put their trust in Jesus are united to him. Where he goes, they go. It is as if we are pulled through the tunnel of death by our trailblazer, Jesus. This unity with him is in fact so close that Paul can even talk about our being 'in Christ'. Our 'participation' in him is what gives us our unshakeable confidence: we know that death will not be the end: 'Now if we died with Christ, we believe that we will also live with him. For we know that since Christ was raised from the dead, he cannot die again; death no longer has mastery over him. The death he died, he died to sin once for all; but the life he lives, he lives to God' (Romans 6:8–10).

Paul takes this even further when he goes on to say that the Spirit of Jesus is living within every Christian. Not only are we living 'with' and 'in' Christ; by his Spirit, he is living in us. We shall consider the impact of this in greater depth in due course; but, for now, notice how Jesus' resurrection grounds our hope: 'if the Spirit of him who raised Jesus from the dead is living in you, he who raised Christ from the dead will also give life to your mortal bodies through his Spirit, who lives in you' (Romans 8:11). This is why Paul can rejoice in his sure hope for the future:

'Death has been swallowed up in victory.'

'Where, O death, is your victory?
Where, O death, is your sting?'

The sting of death is sin, and the power of sin is the law. But thanks be to God! He gives us the victory through our Lord Jesus Christ.
(1 Corinthians 15:54–57)

Words seem insufficient to convey the wonder of this Christ-given confidence. It is a confidence that cannot be shaken, even in the face of tragedy. This was why the great civil-rights leader,

Dr Martin Luther King Jr, was able to console the grieving families of four young black girls bombed by white supremacists while in Sunday school. His words are neither trite nor glib. They merely hold out the hope that Christ's resurrection offers to us all:

> I hope you can find some consolation from Christianity's affirmation that death is not the end. Death is not a period that ends the great sentence of life, but a comma that punctuates it to more lofty significance. Death is not a blind alley that leads the human race into a state of nothingness, but an open door which leads man into life eternal. Let this daring faith, this great invincible surmise, be your sustaining power during these trying days.[8]

The table built up in the previous chapter can now be completed. The final piece in the jigsaw of his achievements during his first coming can be put in place:

Sin's effects		The victory of the cross	Because Christ died as our substitute
We are guilty		*Justification*	Justified by his blood (Rom. 5:9)
We are alienated	HIS DEATH	*Reconciliation*	Brought near through the blood (Eph. 2:13)
We are enslaved		*Redemption*	Redemption through his blood (Eph. 1:7)
We are defiled		*Cleansing*	The blood of Christ ... [will] cleanse (Heb. 9:14)
We are dead		**Resurrection to new life**	If we *died with Christ ...* we will also *live with him* (Rom. 6:8)

A divine demonstration

We are often told that people in the West generally, and university students in particular, are apathetic and indifferent to big causes and problems. While it is certainly true that student-led political demonstrations do not seem as fashionable now as they were in the 1960s, causes and campaigns can still grip the public imagination. Take the anti-capitalism riots in London and Seattle in 2000, or the anti-Iraq war marches that took place around the world in 2003 and 2004. It seems that there are still some things that people feel strongly about, and the whole point of such marches is to make a message heard. Placards and chants are essential to their effectiveness.

The cross is God's placard to his world – this was his demonstration, what one writer called 'God's only self-justification in such a [suffering] world' as ours.[9] It proves that he has an answer to all potential criticisms about his trustworthiness, his goodness or his justice. This is how Paul summarizes it, at two key points in his letter to the Christians in Rome: 'God presented him as a sacrifice of atonement, through faith in his blood. He did this to demonstrate his justice, because in his forbearance he had left the sins committed beforehand unpunished – he did it to demonstrate his justice at the present time, so as to be just and the one who justifies those who have faith in Jesus . . . God demonstrates his own love for us in this: While we were still sinners, Christ died for us' (Romans 3:25–26; 5:8).

God proves two essential characteristics at the cross: his justice and his love. If you struggle to believe that either is true of God, Paul has one piece of advice: 'Look to the cross.' If the twilight of the early hours finds you agonizing over what you can believe about God, your thoughts must take you back to considering the cross. It is at the cross that love and justice can be brought together.

The world without God has no way of doing this. On the one hand it veers towards leniency (if not an unrealistic sentimentality) when it wants to show mercy. Speak to any victims of crime, and they will most likely be crying out for justice. They certainly do not want to be bombarded with extenuating circumstances or excuses so that the culprit's responsibility is explained away. On the other hand, what happens in the face of implacable justice? Justice must be done, but is there no room for mercy and kindness? Is not even the psychopath still a human being with human needs and problems? Bernhard Schlink's narrator faces precisely this difficulty in *The Reader*. Here he articulates his impossible dilemma on discovering that his former lover was guilty of war crimes:

> I wanted simultaneously to understand Hanna's crime and to condemn it. But it was too terrible for that. When I tried to understand, I had the feeling I was failing to condemn it as it must be condemned. When I condemned it as it must be condemned, there was no room for understanding. But even as I wanted to understand Hanna, failing to understand meant betraying her all over again. I could not resolve this. I wanted to pose myself both tasks – understanding and condemnation. But it was impossible to do both.[10]

What the world finds impossible, God solved with breath-taking genius. He must judge because he is holy. He longs to show mercy because of his deep compassion. The solution cost him the life of Jesus, but it demonstrated his complete consistency and faithfulness.

For those who doubt God's love for them personally, the Bible never offers trite platitudes. You may well be infuriated by the habit of Christians smiling weakly with the words 'It's OK – God loves you'; but the Bible never has that tone. Instead, it speaks of God proving and demonstrating his love. When we doubt it, we are not meant to search our deepest feelings for some sense of his love. Instead, we are meant to reassess the fact of his love for us as proved at the cross: 'While we were still sinners, Christ died for us' (Romans 5:8). Ask yourself, 'If Jesus was prepared to die even for me, why should he suddenly give up loving me now? Not only that, how could he have demonstrated his love for me any more fully than through what he did at the cross?' Feeling that God's love is non-existent is never an indication that it is. This is true even in the midst of the most terrible suffering. We naturally assume that pain is caused only by God's suspension or even removal of his care, but this is not the case at all. The cross proves that his love will always be intact for those who respond to him. The cross proves that he can create the maximum good out of the worst the world can do.

How the cross proves God's justice is not immediately obvious, however. The dilemma caused by the truth of Proverbs 17:15 will not go away:

> Acquitting the guilty and condemning the innocent –
>   the LORD detests them both.

How can it be just for us to go free when we really are guilty? How can it be just for Jesus to take the punishment I deserve on to himself? There is certainly mystery here, and we must be careful to avoid assessing God's perfect standards of justice by our inevitably flawed human standards.

One principle of justice, however, has it that the same crime can never be punished twice. That would certainly be unjust. Because Jesus was punished for my sin, I therefore need not be punished. Nevertheless, how can it be just for anyone else to take what I deserve? We need to return to the linked ideas of Jesus' willing *identification with us* and *our participation in him* to answer this. He willingly became fully human, making his identification with us complete, even to the extent that he takes on the ultimate consequences of our sin in our place. When we put our trust in him and are united to him, we then gain his perfect relationship with the Father, which is essentially what it means to have the 'righteousness of God': 'God made him who had no sin to be sin for us, so that in him we might become the righteousness of God'

(2 Corinthians 5:21). Our participation in Christ makes us like the daughter protected from a swarm of bees by a father's enveloping hug. He takes the full force of the stings himself for her. 'Therefore, there is now no condemnation for those who are *in Christ Jesus*' (Romans 8:1; my emphasis).

Most importantly, the cross demonstrates that sin is still serious. God knew that by not bringing judgment sooner, it looked as though the sins committed beforehand would never be punished (see Romans 3:25), but sinners do not get away with it in God's world. There is justice because sin is punished. That punishment is borne either by each individual sinner or by Jesus in substitution for those who come to him for forgiveness; but sin is punished all the same. A suffering and oppressed world that cries out for justice is governed by a God who has proved his determination to bring justice. Like that girl's father, God longs to offer mercy to all who are threatened by his justice, an offer that must be accepted before it can be experienced. Nevertheless, his mercy never undermines his passion for justice.

Summary
Don Carson brilliantly summarizes everything we have been considering in this chapter:

> The cross, then, is the place where God's justice and love meet. God retains the integrity of his justice; God pours out the fullness of his love. In the cross, God shows himself to be just and the one who justifies sinners whose faith rests in his Son. The death of God's own Son is the only adequate gauge of what God thinks of my sin; the death of God's own Son is the only basis on which I may be forgiven that sin. The cross is the triumph of justice and love.[11]

Part 4. Raised to life: so live it!

10. A life made possible

The colossal number of 'self-help' books available today testifies to the fact that millions are dissatisfied. They yearn for improvements to their quality of life, for things to be different, better, more interesting, more fulfilling or more fun. 'How to' guides, addressing every conceivable problem, claim to offer the easiest routes to instant and successful change. But what about personal moral change? Can a self-help book really deliver that simply by motivating people to 'pull their socks up' or persuading them to try out a new technique? So many of us are only too aware that we are not the people we want to be, but have no idea how to change, or even the confidence that such change is ever possible.

Douglas Coupland's characters in *Girlfriend in a Coma* face up to this specific problem. Richard, the narrator, is playing poker with some friends when their conversation starts getting uncomfortable:

'I read about this study,' Wendy said. 'The researchers learned that no matter how hard you tried, the most you could possibly change your personality – your self – was five percent.'

... Wendy's fact made me queasy. The news reminded me of how unhappy I was with who I was at that point. I wanted nothing more than to transform *100* percent.[1]

If Wendy is right, where do we go from there? One option is to hide behind any number of different personalities, for which the virtual world of the Internet offers plenty of scope. You can pretend to be whoever you want to be in cyberspace. The deception can be perfectly concealed until you meet up in 'real space', and even then, it might still be possible to sustain it. 'What's wrong with that?' some might ask. After all, if genuine transformation is out of the question, isn't virtual change the next best thing? Coupland's characters continue:

> A few minutes later, Linus interrupted his poker-faced silence: 'What I notice,' he said, 'is that everybody's kind of accusing everybody else of *acting* these days ... Nobody believes the identities we've made for ourselves. I feel like everybody in the world is fake now – as though people had true cores once, but hucked them away and replaced them with something more attractive but also hollow.'[2]

Later, Richard asks Linus where that outburst came from. His reply is heart-breaking:

> 'I just don't know. I had to say it. I'm worried. I'm worried that we're never going to change. I'm worried that we might not even be *able* to change. Do you ever worry about that?'
> I said, 'Yes.'[3]

The cross forces us to face up to a disturbing reality: we cannot change ourselves. We are enslaved to our sin. However much we would like to change, we cannot alter our inclination to live for ourselves and not God. If this was all there was to Christianity's message for the world, it would be bleak indeed; but it is not. The

Christian message, contrary to many people's impression, is not passed on to make people feel bad. Instead, the only aim is to make us face reality in order to point to the place where real change is possible. For while we cannot change ourselves, the wonderful news is that God can. It has been said that 'if your religion does not change you, then you should change your religion'.[4] Christianity is not about idle theories, unpractical philosophies or dry ideals; it is God's message of revolutionary change. The death of Jesus was designed not merely to stimulate awe or inspiration. Its overarching purpose was to bring us from death to life, from sin to perfection.

Starting out

Having considered some of Jesus' other last words, we come finally to the brief conversation he had with that most surprising of all converts, the crucified thief:

> One of the criminals who hung there hurled insults at him: 'Aren't you the Christ? Save yourself and us!'
>
> But the other criminal rebuked him. 'Don't you fear God,' he said, 'since you are under the same sentence? We are punished justly, for we are getting what our deeds deserve. But this man has done nothing wrong.'
>
> Then he said, 'Jesus, remember me when you come into your kingdom.'
>
> Jesus answered him, 'I tell you the truth, today you will be with me in paradise.'
>
> (Luke 23:39–43)

On the face of it, this conversation did not of course make the slightest difference. There were no magical quick fixes or miraculous rescue plans. Instead, within a short space of time, all three men were dead and their corpses removed – hardly a good advertisement for God's transforming work in people's lives!

If we look beneath the surface, however, we see that, for one man, *everything* had changed: for in those last moments of his life, that thief had become a Christian. We know next to nothing about him. We do not even know his name. Nevertheless, we do know that Jesus accepted his 'death-bed conversion', since that is so much more important than no conversion at all. The real shock is that this categorically proves that being a Christian is not about being 'a good person', but about being a *forgiven* person. The thief did not suddenly become a morally upright person, nor did he prove the genuineness of his conversion through good works. How could he? There was neither the time nor the opportunity! Jesus knew his heart, however, and he knew that the thief had responded to him in two fundamental ways.

Right at the start of his ministry, Jesus established the way someone begins to follow him: 'The time has come ... The kingdom of God is near. Repent and believe the good news!' (Mark 1:15). The kingdom was near because the king, Messiah Jesus, was present. But what did he mean by 'repent and believe'? Both words trip off the tongue so easily, and yet we seldom give them serious thought. The story of the thief on the cross helps us to reconsider them. No-one who responds as the thief did will ever be turned away, regardless of how extreme the circumstances are.

Repentance
While the other criminal exhausted his final breaths firing malicious insults at Jesus, this thief deliberately realigned himself. He refused to participate, but instead rebuked the man. Not only that; he demonstrated some recognition of his own sin. 'Don't you fear God ... since you are under the same sentence? We are punished justly, for we are getting what our deeds deserve. But this man has done nothing wrong.' Most significantly, he puts his final request to Jesus: 'remember me when you come into your kingdom' (Luke 23:40–42).

The *Oxford English Dictionary* defines repentance as feeling 'deep sorrow about one's actions' and resolving 'not to continue a wrongdoing'.[5] While these are certainly true definitions, and may indeed have been true of the thief, they do not tell the whole story. The dictionary unhelpfully omits an essential nuance of the word. A more biblically accurate understanding is to see it as 'a complete turn around', or a 'change of mindset'. It is about recognizing that our previous lifestyle was going in the wrong direction and about doing a U-turn: turning *away* from having myself as Number One, and turning *to* the Creator God, restoring him to the throne of my life. That will inevitably involve an admission of guilt and sorrow for sin, but it must also involve returning to God. For instance, Paul describes the conversion of some Christians he knew as turning 'to God from idols to serve the living and true God' (1 Thessalonians 1:9). If an idol is anything that replaces God as the focus of our life's worship, then sin makes us worship the ultimate idol: ourselves. Repentance rejects utterly such worship. In turning to Jesus for help, the crucified thief indicated his true repentance (verse 42).

Faith
We cannot leave it there, however, since there is another vital ingredient to Jesus' call: faith. Jesus said, 'Repent and *believe* the good news!' Again, faith is much misunderstood these days. How many times do we hear people say, 'I wish I had your faith'? It is presumably meant to be a compliment, but it is an absurd statement. It implies that faith is like a medical condition, except for the fact that this particular condition has benefits! Asking that question proves that the word has drifted from its biblical moorings, since the Bible word translated by 'faith' can equally be translated by 'trust' or 'belief'. You would never say, 'I wish I had your trust.' To that statement, you can only reply with a question: 'What in?' Faith and trust must have an object, since it is impossible simply to 'have faith'. For example, suppose I asked you for a lift in your car. I would then be exercising faith in you and your skills, which may or may not be a wise thing to do. If I knew that you had experienced several crashes in the previous month and that you had had your licence revoked, it would

certainly not be a wise move. If you had just passed your advanced driving test that would be a different matter altogether. It is all a matter of credentials. Are you trustworthy? Are you worthy of my faith?

When Jesus says, 'Repent and believe the good news!' he is forcing us to face a similar issue. Is *he* worthy of our trust? What grounds do we have for trusting *him*? Faith must have this thought-through, reasoned component. Only then can we ask the moral question, namely whether we are actually prepared to trust him with our lives or not. The good news concerns his death on our behalf in order to bring us forgiveness and eternal life. To put our faith in him is simply to take him at his word and trust him to keep it. You do not need to wait for a 'spooky feeling' to be able to have that sort of faith – you merely need to have examined his credentials. Then you take the *step of faith*, acting on what you have decided, just like my getting into your car. This is altogether different from a *leap of faith*. That is a leap into the unknown, a bit like grabbing the first person you see on the street and telling them to drive you home. You can do it if you want to, but it would be stupid because you know nothing about them. While never claiming to provide everything there is to know, the Bible does provide us with everything we need to know in order to assess Jesus' trustworthiness. It promises to make us 'wise for salvation' (2 Timothy 3:15).

Repentance and faith implicitly acknowledge our inability to sort ourselves out. We turn back to Jesus because we know that he is our only hope. That is why the thief's final request is so remarkable. 'Jesus, remember me when you come into your kingdom,' he said (Luke 23:42). He clearly sensed that Jesus still had a future after his death, otherwise he would never have asked! You can dismiss it as an afterlife insurance policy taken out by a desperate man with no alternatives, if you wish. Jesus did not. He knew the man was sincere. He was a man who had repented (realigning himself to Jesus) and believed (trusting Jesus to give him a future). Jesus therefore made him a wonderful promise: 'I tell you the truth, today you will be with me in paradise.' Soon after that, both men were dead; but Luke tells the story because he is confident that the promise came true. His aim in writing was to offer that same confidence to all who would subsequently turn to Jesus. It does not matter what we have done, or when we turn back, as long as we repent and believe.

We need to keep both sides of this coin together, because our constant temptation will be to want one without the other.

What if we repent without believing? This implies that we can save ourselves on our own. It assumes that our sin is not as serious as the Bible claims it is, and that we can somehow make ourselves good enough for God. Everything we have considered so far should undermine this view. We are enslaved to our sin and our guilt. Our deepest needs are forgiveness and new life. Our only hope for them is trusting Jesus' death. As Paul said to those who tried to become right with God (righteous) through keeping the Jewish law, 'if righteousness could be gained through the law, Christ died for nothing!' (Galatians 2:21).

What if we believe without repenting? This also betrays a fundamental misunderstanding. God's plan was always to restore the damage done to his world by the fall, so that everything is brought back into line with its Creator. Jesus died so that we could re-enter his kingdom with him as our king – which means surrendering to him as Lord the throne of our lives. That is effectively what happens when we repent. To assume that we do not need to repent implies an appalling presumption, namely that we can take what God gives us, including forgiveness and future hope, without showing the slightest change in lifestyle. That is in fact the essence of sin: living in God's world with his blessings, without dependence on him. The irony is that this proves that either we do not actually believe the message of the cross, or we do not understand Jesus' sacrifice for us.

We have one final question to address here: *If it was OK for the thief on the cross, why can't I wait until just before my death to turn back?* While it is true that God accepts people at *any* point in their lives because of what Jesus achieved at the cross, there are serious flaws with this logic. Who can say when they will die? Who knows whether they will have time to repent and believe? Who knows whether they will actually *want* to repent and believe? After being Number One for so long, why would anyone suddenly want to change the habit of a lifetime? Not only is there uncertainty about these questions; there is also the fact that to delay after understanding what God offers us is the height of insolence. He sacrificed his Son for our sake. How could we possibly delay responding to him any longer?

Heading home

The observant will have noticed that we still have a serious conundrum here. If it is true to say that we are enslaved to our sin, why would we ever want to repent and believe in the first place? Surely the whole point of sin is that we are content with our addiction. We like sitting on the throne. Our heart is the origin of our sin, and we cannot change that. Worse still, we have already seen that the real disaster of sin is that it kills us spiritually. In Paul's words, we are 'dead' in our 'transgressions and sins' (Ephesians 2:1). How, then, was it possible for the thief on the cross to repent and believe? How is it possible for any of us to do so, when what we need is a new heart and a new life?

Fortunately for us, a new life and a new heart are precisely what we receive when we are united with Jesus. The key to grasping this is Jesus' resurrection: because of that, we have confidence for our own resurrection. Paul tells the Romans, 'If we have been united with him . . . in his death, we will certainly also be united with him in his resurrection' (Romans 6:5). Not only did Jesus die for us, therefore; he also carried us through the barriers of death and separation from God, protecting us *en route* to life beyond death. We participate in his resurrection. The reason this sometimes seems so fanciful is that we expect immediate change at conversion. 'Where is this resurrection?' we are desperate to ask. 'I don't feel particularly different.'

This is an understandable reaction, but the Bible is not a head-in-the-clouds book. It is down to earth and full of realism. The New Testament writers are deeply concerned to prepare us for the normal experience of being Christian. They are convinced that we do participate in Christ's resurrection, but make it clear that we appropriate the full benefits of it in a three-stage process: what we might call the three tenses of our resurrection.

Past resurrection: regeneration
We hear much talk of the need for inner-city regeneration or rebirth in districts that have all but died. Those with wealth have moved out to the suburbs, while those who remain in the centre have little or no hope for employment or a future. This is a pressing social issue that must be addressed. If that seems an intractable dilemma, however, there is another form of regeneration that everyone, whether wealthy or poverty-stricken, needs in order to have hope. This is even more difficult to achieve.

Early on in his ministry, Jesus had a strange conversation with the learned Jewish scholar Nicodemus:

> Jesus declared, 'I tell you the truth, no-one can see the kingdom of God unless he is born again.'
> 'How can a man be born when he is old?' Nicodemus asked. 'Surely he cannot enter a second time into his mother's womb to be born!'
> '... You should not be surprised at my saying, "You must be born again." The wind blows wherever it pleases. You hear its sound, but you cannot tell where it comes from or where it is going. So it is with everyone born of the Spirit.'
> (John 3:3–4, 7–8)

Nicodemus's great learning did not prevent his confusion at this. He asked Jesus about re-entering a mother's womb, not because he actually believed it to be possible, but because he thought Jesus was spouting nonsense. What a stupid idea! Jesus was not joking, however, but was teaching a vital truth: *everyone* needs a second birth. You cannot follow him without being born again. The shock for Nicodemus was that even he, the upright and devout scholar, was included.

As in the case of the patient on the transplant waiting list, there is only one cure: the substitution of a fresh, new heart for the dying heart. That is the only hope for life. No amount of willpower will repair the damage; nor is this an operation that you can perform on yourself! It needs the skilled hands of experts. This is precisely what God offers us when he sends his Spirit. He brings us the fruits of Christ's resurrection as he brings us to spiritual life. As Paul continues in the Ephesians passage referred to above, God in his mercy 'made us alive with Christ even when we were dead in transgressions – it is by grace you have been saved' (Ephesians 2:5).

The Spirit is not some strange life-force or energy field, but is personal. He is 'another' like Jesus, the key difference being that he is not bound by time or space. Among his New Testament titles are 'Spirit of God and Christ', the 'Spirit of Jesus' and the 'Spirit of God's Son'.[6] His role is to bring glory to Jesus (John 16:14), which is done supremely when people come to repentance and faith in Jesus. He enables that to happen because he breathes new life into them. The heart is transformed, thus revolutionizing their spiritual orientation. Instead of being self-centred, they begin to be Jesus-centred. As a former minister of mine used to say, 'The Holy Spirit is not given to us to make the Christian life easy. He is given to us to make the Christian life possible.'

The effects of storms are obvious: trees blocking streets, floods rising above record levels, boats tossed about on mammoth waves. Nevertheless, we cannot see the wind that has these effects; it is invisible, which is why children have such fun leaning into it. They look as though they are being propped up by some strange force. The Spirit is similarly invisible to the human eye, but his work is unmistakable to the human heart. He cannot be tied down or manipulated, but he will bring about the wonder of new birth wherever he sees fit. He is constantly at his work of bringing glory to Jesus.

This second birth will not necessarily feel any different, however. When people first repent and believe the good news, they are often disappointed at the lack of a 'zap' or overwhelming emotion. People do sometimes have strong emotions when they first experience the joys of forgiveness and hope; but they are not specifically promised. What will certainly happen is that desires and priorities will gradually start to change. For instance, 'Christ' will no longer be a swear word, and there will be the new desire to meet with other Christians, priorities that were perhaps insignificant before. These are signs of the wind-like Spirit of Jesus starting his work, signs of the resurrection to spiritual life.

This whole concept will worry some and offend others. If our regeneration is all the Spirit's work, surely the only logical thing we can do is to wait until we are 'zapped'. Jesus' aim was not to direct us into passive complacency, but to remind us of our total dependence on God for our rescue. We are not meant to rest on our laurels with the excuse that we have not been given this new birth by the Spirit. However hard it is to get our minds round this idea, the fact that Jesus calls us to repent and believe implies that we are responsible for our actions. The Bible simply describes a world where God's sovereign control and humanity's responsibility for its actions are compatible ideas. I cannot understand how that works, but I know that both are true of my own conversion. I know that becoming a Christian is something that I wanted to do. As I look back, I also know that I could never have done it without God's intervention. This is not something to worry about. Instead, it is something to be immensely grateful for. Furthermore, if you have not come to Christ yourself, what is there to stop you praying to God for that new birth?

There is one vital aspect of our regeneration that we still need to consider. Returning to Ephesians 2, Paul continues with a startling statement: 'And God raised us up with Christ and seated us with him in the heavenly realms in Christ Jesus' (Ephesians 2:6).

Because of this truth Jesus was able to make such a promise to the thief on the cross. There may not have been major changes in how he felt as he hung there, but at his repentance and faith he was spiritually raised and given a place in heaven. Because we go where Jesus goes if we are 'in him', and because he is now seated in heaven with his mission accomplished, it is as if we are there as well. Although we are not yet physically present in heaven, we dwell in heaven spiritually because that is where Christ is. It is as if there is already a seat there with our names on it. This is what gives us confidence for the future. We have a new home and our lives are now spent heading home. It just so happens that most of us have to wait longer than the crucified thief had to wait before reaching our destination.

There are strong similarities here with the achievements of the cross that we have already thought through. Notice the connection to our justification: God's declaration of our innocence. He now sees us as perfect, with Christ's righteousness, just as he sees us as raised in Christ to heaven. There is also the link to our adoption as sons of God. Regeneration effectively marks the signing of our adoption papers. We are declared perfect, but we are not perfect yet. We are adopted into God's family, but we do not fully display the family likeness yet. We are raised to heaven, but we are not there yet. There is some serious catching up to do with our new-found status, which is why we need to consider our present process of resurrection.

Present resurrection: mortification

Christians keep on sinning. If you are a Christian and that fact is not obvious to you, you can be sure that it is obvious to those around you! That is why we are so often accused of hypocrisy. We come across as actors, giving the impression that our lives match our message, when all along the reality is starkly different. Two examples have brought this home to me powerfully.

A few years ago, I went to a Christian bookshop in London in order to buy a biblical commentary. I discovered that the entire series was available only from assistants behind the counter because, over a period of months, various volumes had been disappearing. It is hard to imagine that anyone other than a Bible student or even a pastor would want to collect that particular series, so it seems we must assume that it was a Christian who was stealing the volumes.

In the early summer of 2000, the sporting world was stunned by revelations of match-fixing by none other than Hansie Cronjé, captain of the South African cricket team. While some found the mere fact that this went on in professional cricket shocking, the most depressing aspect to the scandal was that Cronjé had been a keen, professing Christian for years. He was both a role model and a powerful witness to the joy of knowing Christ's forgiveness. How could he of all people get himself disgraced in that way?

You need only the briefest of glances at church history to see the most appalling things done in the name of Jesus. They cannot be condoned and sometimes they cannot easily be explained. The phenomenon of Christians *continuing* to sin therefore causes many people to conclude that the resurrection change that God brings about in our lives is a mere pipe-dream. Paul claimed that 'we . . . are being transformed into his likeness with everincreasing glory, which comes from the Lord, who is the Spirit' (2 Corinthians 3:18). Is this credible? If the Christian religion does not bring about the change it promises, should we not discard that as well? Is there no alternative to the despair of Douglas Coupland's poker players?

If we understood the moral resurrection that needs to take place in a Christian's life, however, we would not be surprised by this. Paul expects Christians to sin, and so we need to dissect some of his thinking to see why this is the case. He writes to the Roman Christians:

> You, however, are controlled not by the sinful nature but by the Spirit, if the Spirit of God lives in you. And if anyone does not have the Spirit of Christ, he does not belong to Christ. But if Christ is in you, your body is dead because of sin, yet your spirit is alive

because of righteousness. And if the Spirit of him who raised Jesus from the dead is living in you, he who raised Christ from the dead will also give life to your mortal bodies through his Spirit, who lives in you. Therefore, brothers, we have an obligation – but it is not to the sinful nature, to live according to it.

(Romans 8:9–12)

We find ourselves in an 'in-between' time. We have been raised to new life – Christ lives in us and we have spiritual life, having been given his righteousness (verse 10). Nevertheless, our bodies are still dead (verse 10) – we have not been raised to full physical and moral perfection yet. This sets up a conflict within us: our sinful nature against the Spirit. There is a battle that rages between what we want to do and what we ought to do, between our own selfish desires and God's desires for us. The Spirit's aim is to put our sinful desires to death – which is why this process is described as mortification – but we are so attached to our sin that the battle can sometimes be intense. Paul expresses it even more starkly when he refers to a crucifying of 'the sinful nature with its passions and desires' (Galatians 5:24). Christ was crucified for us so that we could be free from the power of sin. Paul is telling us to be ruthless in our treatment of it. We can hope to do this only by the power of the Spirit.

Some find the reality of this conflict highly discouraging. The fact that people battle with sin, perhaps even a sin that continually recurs, can lead them to doubt whether or not the new birth has happened at all. 'Where is the evidence of it in my life?' they ask. 'Where is the resurrection power of the Spirit in my life? It seems non-existent at times!' Some even testify to feeling that they have actually become *worse*, not better! What is going on?

We need to turn these questions on their head, because Paul tells us to expect conflict. He maintains that conflict with sin is *normal* Christian experience. Why else would he conclude in that Romans passage that 'we have an obligation'? His assumption is that what we *ought to do* is still not necessarily what we *want to do*, even after we have become Christians. While he makes it clear that we should expect to fight, he never says the fight is easy, but that it is unavoidable. This is how he puts it for the Galatian Christians: 'So I say, live by the Spirit, and you will not gratify the desires of the sinful nature. For the sinful nature desires what is contrary to the Spirit, and the Spirit what is contrary to the sinful nature. They are in conflict with each other, so that you do not do what you want' (Galatians 5:16–17).

Moral conflict is therefore normal Christian experience; but not only is it normal, it is also a great encouragement. The simple fact that there is conflict indicates that the Spirit is present in the first place. If he was not, why would we ever seek to go God's way and not our own in the daily decisions of life? The Spirit is constantly urging us to fight our sin, which means that the experience of this conflict should not lead to despair. On the contrary, our task is to co-operate with every fibre of our being in this battle. When we have been brought into God's family, our deepest desire should be to be transformed into the family likeness. That is what becoming holy is all about, as we seek to become more like our holy and perfect Father in heaven. It is not a matter of sitting back and letting the Spirit take the strain; nor is it a matter of the Spirit constantly telling us to 'pull our socks up'. It is 100% effort from both sides. As Paul urged the Philippians, 'continue to work out your salvation with fear and trembling, for it is God who works in you' (Philippians 2:12–13). That we do not co-operate in this way explains why Christians still sin.

If we sense a deterioration in our holiness, that may well be because we are simply aware of more areas in our lives that previously we had not attended to. This is why people who have been Christians for decades are still aware of their sin, and yet when we meet them, they radiate Christlikeness. There has been substantial change in their lives, but they are more attuned to the work that remains to be done.

Our sin, therefore, should not necessarily cast doubt on our status as justified people. That status was won at the cross. If repeated sin concerns you, that in itself is a good sign. It demonstrates that you share God's concern for your life, which is his plan to make you more like him. The important thing when we do sin is to return to God as soon as possible, to turn away from our sin (a 'mini-repentance' if you like) and trust his saving work in Jesus (a 'mini-believing'). It is not that we are being converted all over again, but that we are like the adopted son who has had an unjustified argument with his father. The fact of his family membership is not in question; it is just that the father–son relationship has soured somewhat. The child has only to apologize for good terms to be resumed. That is why there is great wisdom in John Stott's often-repeated suggestion that we should therefore 'daily bewail our sin and daily adore our Saviour'. Doing this will ensure that we keep on good terms with our heavenly Father. If you have no concern at all for the sin in your life, there is a genuine cause for alarm. You must reassess whether or not you understand the Christian message at all. If you are concerned for sin, however, you can have all the confidence in the world that God will be pleased to hear from you.

Future resurrection: perfection

Heaven seems an insubstantial place to most people. On a recent edition of the BBC's *Fantasy Rooms*, where guests challenge designers to realize their interior-design dreams, one guest asked for her bedroom to be made like heaven.[7] This was the first time the designer had been asked to do this, and it forced him to do some serious thinking. Everyone's perception of heaven is bound to be different, and so he wanted to be sure he knew what the guest was really asking. He asked her, 'Is it angels? Is it pearly gates? Is it fluffy clouds? What do you want?' As it turned out, he ended up painting an evening sky filled with fluffy clouds and a few twinkling stars. As an example of interior design it was highly effective, but as an attempt at theological speculation it was a disaster!

While never giving us a map to locate or guide us through heaven, the Bible does give us some clues as to what it is like. The vital thing is that it is a real and material place, where God's people will be in the presence of God himself. It is a Christian's true home, as tangible as any place we might call home in this life. Jesus' own resurrection helps us to anticipate what we shall experience at our eventual resurrection to our heavenly home.

Above all, the most noticeable aspect of Jesus' resurrection body was that it was physical. All four Gospel writers insist on his resurrection being bodily, which is why they all go to such lengths to emphasize that Jesus' tomb really was empty – his body had to be somewhere else (for example, John 20:1–9)! That is why Luke describes Jesus as walking along a road and chatting to fellow-travellers. Read the account of it in Luke 24 and notice how Cleopas and his partner see nothing out of the ordinary in their companion. Then John describes Jesus physically appearing to all his closest disciples in John 20 – 21. He is clearly the one who has been crucified: his wounds are still visible. He is even able to share in a barbecue breakfast on the beach (20:27; 21:12–15). This is no ghost!

This is not to say that everything remained the same. Notice the way John describes one of Jesus' earlier visits to his friends. 'On the evening of that first day of the week, when the disciples were together, with the doors locked for fear of the Jews, Jesus came and stood among them and said, "Peace be with you!"' (John 20:19). Why mention the locked doors if not to imply that Jesus was somehow able to appear without the need to open them? The point is that Jesus' body was not so much less than physical as more than physical. That is hard to understand, but it is not surprising for a world beyond ours to have incomprehensible qualities. Jesus broke into this world with a hint of the nature of the next.

When Paul indicates that the day will come when we shall be made perfect, we should therefore take Jesus' experience into account: 'We will not all sleep, but we will all be changed – in a flash, in the twinkling of an eye, at the last trumpet. For the trumpet will sound, the dead will be raised imperishable, and we will be changed' (1 Corinthians 15:51–52).

This will happen on the day we die or the day of Christ's return, whichever happens first. It is the ultimate change; the sort of transformation that we yearn for and yet perhaps feel is too much of a fantasy. Yet Paul promised to the Philippian Christians that 'he who began a good work in you will carry it on to completion until the day of Christ Jesus' (Philippians 1:6). This is God's work and, because of that, we can be sure it will happen. The day will come when his will for our lives will be accomplished. We shall truly be like our heavenly Father. On that day, we shall be able to enjoy all the joys of being with God and his global family for eternity. Just as Jesus' resurrection body had both continuities and discontinuities with his former body, so shall ours. The ultimate difference is that we shall never have to face the battle against sin, decay or death again. This is hardly a 'fluffy clouds' view of heaven – quite the opposite, in fact. This is *more* tangible even than physical reality, with moral perfection attained at last.

At the centre of it all will be our Saviour and Lord – Jesus Christ. Heaven is about relationships being enjoyed, which is why one biblical picture of heaven is a marriage feast: a wonderful family get-together on the most awesome scale. Because it is a family fully sharing the likeness of the head of the family, there will be none of the tensions we might normally associate with large family gatherings. Instead, there will be perfect harmony as people from every continent, every social background, every intellectual ability, every conceivable human subgroup are all brought together in one society. That almost seems too good to be true; but it is not too good to be true, since the truth is even better than we could possibly imagine. We shall be home!

Is it any wonder, then, that we get frustrated in this life? If heaven is where we belong, but are not yet present, are we surprised that we are impatient for it? A sense of frustration is normal Christian experience. If we do not sense it, we presumably do not yet belong in heaven. As Paul wrote to the Romans, 'we ourselves, who have the firstfruits of the Spirit, groan inwardly as we wait eagerly for our adoption as sons, the redemption of our bodies' (Romans 8:23). That is our hope. That is what we long for. We have the guarantee of it happening – the firstfruits were the first indication of the calibre of the coming harvest. The transforming work of the Spirit is just the beginning – the best is yet to come!

This is a truly wonderful transformation, to which we can look forward. Not only are we forgiven but we have the sure hope of being changed, a change beyond the wildest dreams of Coupland's characters. This is change that God offers to every one of us.

Summary

The table below summarizes what we receive when we repent and believe the good news.

Resurrection tense	Our experience	God's family
Past resurrection – our conversion	*Regeneration* or *second birth*	We are reborn into God's new family
Present resurrection – our conflict	*Mortification* or *crucifying the sinful nature*	We increasingly take on the family likeness
Future resurrection – our conviction	*Perfection* or *complete 'Christlikeness'*	We are united with the whole family of God

11. A cross-shaped life

Please read Mark 8:22–38 and Philippians 2

Cults terrify us. Their control over people is absolute, their existence almost inexplicable, and yet not a year goes by without reports of some new cult-related tragedy. In 1997 the Heaven's Gate cult committed group suicide in order to join the Hale Bopp comet, which would apparently take them into paradise after its journey past Earth. More alarmingly still, there was the news that emerged from south-west Uganda during March 2000. More than a thousand members of the 'Movement for the Restoration of the Ten Commandments of God' were initially thought to have committed suicide after prophecies of the end of the world failed to come true. As more evidence came to light in the village of Kanungu, however, it became clear that many had been massacred. This made it the largest cult death toll ever, even outstripping the grisly 1978 record of Jim Jones's Guyana cult. Before their tragic deaths, members were passionately committed to their new beliefs. The power of their leaders, Joseph Kibwetere and the former prostitute 'Sister' Credonia Mwerinde, was such that members surrendered everything they owned, husbands and wives agreed not to live together, and many gave up speaking altogether, communicating instead by sign language. Why will people do such things? How do we prevent them recurring?

One contemporary response is to avoid extreme commitments or fanaticism altogether. If we reject absolutely all claims to absolute truth, if we never allow ourselves to be subject to extreme authoritarian control, and if we attempt to live life on our own terms and no-one else's, then we shall be safe. People we meet may not express their apathy in quite these terms, but it is what many people feel. To be passionate about a cause or, worse still, a mere belief, is bound to lead to disaster – or so we are led to believe.

The problem is that this leads to a collision course with the claims of Christianity. Jesus placed high – some would say unreasonably high – demands on those who follow him. In the light of Kanungu, however, these demands actually seem dangerous. Was Jesus no more than the mastermind behind a uniquely successful cult? That may seem absurd after centuries of institutional Christianity. Nevertheless, Jesus demanded nothing less than total, even fanatical, allegiance. How are we to decide whether it is safe, let alone right, to submit to him? Before answering that, we must ask what his demands are, and what grounds he has for making them.

Follow Christ

The disciples took a while to accept that Jesus was God's anointed king. Yet even when they did, they had no real understanding of what that meant. When Peter blurted out that Jesus was indeed 'the Christ', he naturally assumed that it meant that Jesus was going places (Mark 8:29). After all, a human being can attain no higher distinction than God's Messiah or Christ. Immediately after Peter's public realization, however, Jesus dropped two bombshells into the conversation. The first was simple: in order to complete his God-given mission as the Christ, he must die: 'He [Jesus] then began to teach them that the Son of Man must suffer many things and be rejected by the elders, chief priests and teachers of the law, and that he must be killed and after three days rise again' (Mark 8:31).

Execution at the hands of God's very own people was not exactly what one would expect for God's king. Jesus did not anticipate earthly glory or battle honours worthy of a monarch. Instead, he looked ahead to shame, agony and death. No wonder Peter objected. He 'took him [Jesus] aside and began to rebuke him' (Mark 8:32). That was no way for a king to go. Peter's audacity led to one of Jesus' most spine-chilling outbursts: 'But when Jesus turned and looked at his disciples, he rebuked Peter. "Get behind me, Satan!" he said. "You do not have in mind the things of God but the things of men" ' (Mark 8:33).

Minutes before, Peter had made the momentous confession of Jesus' identity. Now he was condemned in the bluntest terms imaginable. He was tempting Jesus to disobey God in favour of an easier option, which was precisely what Satan had tried during the forty days in the wilderness (Matthew 4:1–11). Jesus was clear: the Son of Man *must* suffer ... *must* be rejected ... *must* be killed ... *must* rise again.

Jesus then drops the second bombshell: not only must God's king be prepared to die; his subjects must be as well. Jesus has called on people to follow him countless times before, of course, but only now does he spell out what that means: 'If anyone would come after me, he must deny himself and take up his cross and follow me. For whoever wants to save his life will lose it, but whoever loses his life for me and for the gospel will save it. What good is it for a man to gain the whole world, yet forfeit his soul?' (Mark 8:34–37).

Jesus is not asking his followers to take on the mantle of Messiah themselves, since that would be both absurd and impossible. He is simply calling for them to follow in his footsteps.

Crucifixion was a criminal's death, the result of a court's decision to rid civilized society of its unworthy members. The criminal was then paraded before malicious crowds, bent beneath the wooden crossbeam, to the place of execution. Jesus certainly experienced that. Following him therefore means being prepared both to identify with that shame and humiliation and to walk on the path to crucifixion. Banish for ever all notions of 'a cross to bear', implying having to put up with awkward great-aunts or demanding responsibilities at work. Jesus is ultimately asking people to *die*. We have too easily domesticated his call. The scandal of his demand is only truly apparent when we draw on the imagery used in chapter 2 and translate it in these terms: 'Bear the shame of your "burning-tyre necklace" if you want to follow me.'

At the heart of this call is the need for people to 'deny self' (Mark 8:34). The context must determine what the phrase means, because many have assumed all kinds of unhelpful things from it. Self-interest and personal desires are not to control us any longer. Jesus is saying, 'You must remove the crown of your life from your own head and hand it back to me – I am the boss now. I must come first.' Self-denial is not about losing your identity or sense of personal worth. We have already seen how these need to be grounded upon the knowledge that we have been redeemed by the blood of Jesus. As William Temple put it, 'My worth is what I am worth to God; and that is a marvellous great deal, for Christ died for me.'[1] In the confidence of such extravagant love, we are then able to surrender to him willingly. True self-denial is seen when I surrender first place in my life to Jesus. That was never going to come easily, for his call runs counter to the way we naturally think. Jesus made the cost very clear. Few of us deliberately seek to make things harder for ourselves, yet that is effectively what Jesus demands of *all* his followers. 'If *anyone* would come after me, he must deny himself and take up his cross and follow me' (Mark 8:34; my emphasis).

Dietrich Bonhoeffer took this call seriously. He began his ministry in 1928 and so found himself working in and out of Germany at a time when the Nazi party was beginning its ascent to power. He was outspoken in his opposition to its values and vision, which culminated in his execution only three weeks before the war's end. He once said, 'When God calls a man, he bids him come and die,' and it was a principle he lived by throughout his ministry. One commentator on his life and thought wrote this:

> If we ask why Bonhoeffer had the courage to be martyred, we can only answer that he died many times before he was hanged at the concentration camp in Flossenburg. He was passionately convinced that discipleship meant death – death to our own comforts, death to our own agendas, and when necessary, physical death too. The cross of Christ was a symbol of that death and could never be confused with a swastika, which was a symbol of man's quest for life.[2]

Bonhoeffer understood what it meant to die to self. It was the non-negotiable heart of discipleship. Consequently, he was fiercely critical of his contemporaries who kept a deliberately low profile during the Nazis' expanding regime. He felt that they were too quick to accommodate Nazism into Christianity, often for the sake of 'having a quiet life'.

Hitler demanded nothing less than unqualified allegiance, which deliberately put him in conflict with Jesus Christ. Bonhoeffer therefore felt he had no option but to resist the Führer. It was merely an outworking of his discipleship of Jesus. Contemporaries undoubtedly argued that opposing a totalitarian regime is not politically astute. Work with it and try to change it, they might have said. Bonhoeffer realized, however, that Christ does not call us to be politically astute. He is calling us to follow him to the death, if it must come to that. Such a call may sound like stupidity or wastefulness. Yet in spite of whatever suffering and difficulty Jesus calls us to endure, it is still worth it. There is life after death; this world is not all there is.

The prospect of an eternal future gives Jesus' challenge its rationale: 'What good is it for a man to gain the whole world, yet forfeit his soul?' he asked (Mark 8:36). The answer is obvious, and yet Jesus' question is one that many attempt to sidestep for fear of the possible consequences. In total contrast to that mentality of self-delusion, a Christian knows that 'whoever loses his life for me and for the gospel will save it' (Mark 8:35). The long-term benefits of doing this are incalculable. To underline this, another twentieth-century martyr, Jim Elliot, wrote several years before his early death in 1956, 'He is no fool who gives what he cannot keep to gain what he cannot lose.'[3] Being prepared to surrender one's rights to life now is surely a price worth paying for life in the world to come; but pay it we must. For no-one can follow Jesus into heaven without following him past the cross. What he was prepared to do for us, we must be prepared to do for him. The preacher Charles Spurgeon summed it up brilliantly: 'There are no crown-wearers in heaven who were not cross-bearers here below.'

Jesus' unambiguous challenge gives people cold feet. Not only his claims are preposterous, they say; so are his demands. What is the difference between what he expects and promises, and what a modern cult preaches? Before members of the Heaven's Gate cult willingly followed their leader into death, they left behind eerie video testimonies and a website that is still accessible. Their vision is expressed in strange language, but you cannot miss the point: 'By the time you receive this, we'll be gone. We came from the Level Above Human in distant space and we have now exited the bodies that we were wearing for our earthly task, to return to the world from whence we came – task completed.'

It goes on to say: 'If the above information is *consumed* or *assimilated*, you may experience such side effects as loss of marriage, family, friends, career, respectability and credibility. Continued use could even result in the loss of your membership in the human kingdom.'[4]

Its peculiar jargon aside, does this not ring familiar bells? Heaven's Gate demands total subservience despite the antagonism that it will cause among family and friends. So what is the difference between Heaven's Gate and Jesus?

The key lies in who Jesus was and what he came to do. These questions have of course been the subject of this whole book. Yet the critical issue here is Jesus' character. He was sinless and holy.

He was totally trustworthy, such that people from all walks of life and social backgrounds were prepared to put their trust in him. Jesus was no deranged madman or cynical con-artist. After all, the biggest difficulty his opponents had at his trial was to amass evidence against him, which is why they were forced to rely on fabricated evidence (Mark 14:55–56; cf. Luke 23:14). Here was no flawed, egotistical cult leader. What is more, no cult leader would ever have submitted to a mission like Jesus'. A cult leader would never willingly endure what Jesus endured. He did not go to the cross as a PR stunt or to get on the front pages; he went there out of a deep love for his Father and for us.

The clinching argument, however, is that Jesus, unlike any cult leader, could back up his claims. When Peter confessed to Jesus, 'You are the Christ,' it was not a bolt from the blue (Mark 8:29). There were good grounds for believing it. Credonia Mwerinde and Joseph Kibwetere saw their authority disintegrate when the world's end failed to materialize. They were thus exposed as false prophets. In total contrast, Jesus' credibility was not destroyed by his own death but was instead grounded on it, because he had predicted its necessity. Then his resurrection from death vindicated his claims to be God's Son and king. Jesus never made groundless or arrogant demands for allegiance. He uniquely had the authority of God. He was not someone you could dismiss as a crank or a charlatan. He demanded to be taken seriously, because the consequences for not doing so are serious: 'If anyone is ashamed of me and my words in this adulterous and sinful generation, the Son of Man will be ashamed of him when he comes in his Father's glory with the holy angels' (Mark 8:38).

When he calls on us to take up our cross, he is therefore expecting of us no more than he expected of himself. How can we *not* respond by surrendering our whole lives to him in return? That is the only appropriate response to someone who has given everything for us. However, we must take this further. For in Christ, we have the perfect model for how to live in God's world. It's all a question of attitude.

Imitate Christ

If our society is fanatical about anything, it is rights. The growing concern for human rights in recent decades is crucial to rooting out and preventing terrible injustice around the world. If we ever found ourselves or close relatives unjustly imprisoned for political or religious beliefs, which of us would not be profoundly grateful for organizations like Amnesty International? Not only that; the core values of social justice are grounded in the biblical belief in a God who loathes injustice. It is profoundly Christian to be concerned for the poor and oppressed. However, we must be aware of the impact of all the talk of rights. Rights have been extended to include nearly everything. We have consumer rights, hospital-patient rights, train-passenger rights, the right to have a baby, the right to be happy. Again, if it is a question of combating injustice and inequality, this sort of language has a vital role. In the West, however, it has generated a potentially dangerous and unhealthy attitude. We have shifted from a concern for the rights of *others* to what *I* can get for myself. We yearn for more of everything, by right. We expect to be able to put our own needs first, by right. We want to be able to make up the rules for our own lives, by right. That of course takes us to the heart of sin. As we have already seen, that was precisely the allure of the fruit on the tree of the knowledge of good and evil in Genesis 3. The temptation 'to be like God' was too strong to resist, for sin is about wanting to be a god in my own life, by right.

In the light of this, we are faced with a conundrum when we come to Paul's letter to the Philippians. Having just said that trying to be like God is the ultimate sin, we find that Paul says to his readers, 'Your attitude should be the same as that of Christ Jesus' (Philippians 2:5). In effect, he tells them to be like God! So what is the difference between Genesis 3 and Philippians 2? There is all the difference in the world, and the answer can be summarized simply: it is the difference between humanity's way of trying to be God, and God's way of being God. Instead of

Satan's quick-fix route to being 'like God', Paul tells us that we ought to be what God is really like.

The God who gave up his rights

Whether Paul wrote this poem himself, or borrowed it from another, it is a wonderful summary of the life of Jesus. This is the first part:

> [Christ Jesus], being in very nature God,
>> did not consider equality with God something to be grasped,
>
> but made himself nothing,
>> taking the very nature of a servant,
>>
>> being made in human likeness.
>
> And being found in appearance as a man,
>> he humbled himself
>>
>> and became obedient to death – even death on a cross!
>
> (Philippians 2:6–8)

Notice where the poem begins. It does not start with Christmas, as Matthew and Luke do in their Gospels. It does not even start with Old Testament prophecies. It is far bolder, for it starts with the mind of God in heaven. Paul is explicit in his belief that Jesus was divine – he was 'in very nature God'. Furthermore, notice the character of God in that verse. We rightly associate God with power, authority and knowledge, and yet Jesus 'did not consider equality with God something to be grasped'. The issue is not so much the fact of Jesus' equality with the Father in heaven, as what he did with his equality. He did not consider his divinity something to be taken advantage of or exploited for his own ends. In other words, he did not stand on his rights. Why? The answer is simple: because he 'was in very nature God'. That is what God is like. He is not a grabbing or grasping God. He is the exact opposite – a giving God.

This was made plain for the whole world to see when God the Son became incarnate. More than that, he went straight to the bottom of the pile, as a man with no rights at all. He became a slave! '[He] made himself nothing, taking the very nature of a servant, being made in human likeness.' 'Servant' is far too polite a translation, because it makes us think of butlers in period dramas. 'Slave' is far more accurate. And although in the world's eyes Jesus became 'a nothing', this was his deliberate purpose.

We can hardly imagine what that must have meant for him. We have no idea, because we have no conception of how glorious heaven must be. It was an incredible descent. A man with an experience that allows us the smallest glimpse of how agonizing that must have been for Jesus is Primo Levi, although his descent was never voluntary. He was a highly trained industrial chemist who ended up in Auschwitz during the war. In his heart-breaking book *If This Is a Man* he describes what it meant to have been 'something' only to become 'nothing' in the eyes of his SS guards.

> They hear us speak in many languages, which they do not
> understand and which sound to them as grotesque as animal
> noises; they see us reduced to ignoble slavery, without hair,
> without honour and without names, beaten every day, more
> abject every day, and they never see in our eyes a light of
> rebellion, or of peace, or of faith. They know us as thieves
> and untrustworthy, muddy, ragged and starving, and mistaking
> the effect for the cause, they judge us worthy of our abasement.
> Who of them could tell one of our faces apart from
> another?[5]

That is what it is like to be a slave: ignored, abused and oppressed. No wonder Levi entitled his book *If This Is a Man*, because he was not treated like a man. Levi's running theme is the bitter cruelty of being treated as an animal. Yet, when we look at the poem in Philippians, the big question is, 'Is this a God?' Can this really be God's Messiah?

Paul does not stop there.

The God on death row

> And being found in appearance as a man,
>   he humbled himself
>   and became obedient to death – even death on a cross!
> (Philippians 2:8)

This follows on from the previous point. Because the Nazis treated millions as vermin, they had no qualms about genocide. To them human life was worthless. Countless innocent people found themselves on death row through no fault of their own, and to be on death row is to be the ultimate society reject. But Jesus did it deliberately: 'He humbled himself' out of obedience. He refused to defend himself, even when he had the chance. He gave up the right even to live. Not only that, as we have seen already; he gave up his ultimate right: the right to a relationship with his Father. To say he humbled himself seems like an understatement. He became society's outcast, and the Father's outcast. The reason for this? As we have seen time and time again throughout this book, he surrendered himself for us. He gave up his rights, so that we might have 'the right to become children of God' (John 1:12).

I gather that if you go to Union Seminary in Yeotmal, India, you enter a courtyard that contains a statue guaranteed to make you think. The focus is on a tall, dignified figure, someone you would naturally identify as an important religious figure. He is obviously worthy of respect, not least because hunched before him is a menial slave. Any good Hindu, let alone Christian, would accept this as right and proper, until they actually read the small inscription beneath it: 'Jesus washing Peter's feet', based on John 13. It is breathtaking. Is that your God? Is that the one you adore and worship? Is that the one you seek to imitate? If you want to be like God, that is what you are being called to do. In response to the service he has shown us, we must show service to him and the world, a service that does not stand on its rights. Instead, it asks, 'Where can I help?'

This service will take many forms, which Paul outlines throughout Philippians. So, for example, he instructs them: 'Do nothing out of selfish ambition or vain conceit, but in humility consider others better than yourselves. Each of you should look not only to your own interests, but also to the interests of others' (Philippians 2:3–4).

That is precisely the way Jesus behaved. He has shown us true love. Having experienced it for ourselves, how can we not imitate him and allow others to know what his love is like? From infancy we all imitate others. Having young children around the house brought this home forcefully to us, as we saw them imitating habits and words that we would rather they had never noticed! Paul's major concern in Philippians is that we are careful whom we imitate. Ultimately it must be Christ for the Christian. Otherwise, we will be no different from the world around us. In an age that is so concerned for personal rights this would be disastrous. We are called to 'shine like stars in the universe' (Philippians 2:15), so that others will get a glimpse of what God is really like. A life lived for Jesus, imitating his self-giving love, is a unique testimony to the love that he demonstrated once and for all on the cross.

A Christlike life is not enough on its own; it must be explained, which is why Paul instructs his readers to 'hold out the word of life' (Philippians 2:16). What message could be more glorious than that of the death of Jesus that brings us life? A scientist who discovered the perfect cure for Aids would be considered immoral and cruel if she did not allow it to be published. Jesus has an offer of life far greater than a temporary reprieve from sickness. He offers life with him for eternity. The loving thing to do is to let people know it is available. We cannot have a message without a lifestyle to back it up, or no-one will take us seriously. We cannot have a lifestyle without a message to explain our motivations, or no-one will understand us. We need both. The cross of Christ demands both. At the cross, we find the motive and model for living for others. At the cross, we find the content of the message to pass on to others.

Before I close, there is one final part of the jigsaw to place from Paul's poem. As we know, Jesus' story did not end at the cross.

Worship Christ

> Therefore God exalted him to the highest place
>> and gave him the name that is above every name,
> that at the name of Jesus every knee should bow,
>> in heaven and on earth and under the earth,
> and every tongue confess that Jesus Christ is Lord,
>> to the glory of God the Father.
> (Philippians 2:9–11)

Death was not the end for Jesus. Because he endured the cross out of total obedience to the Father, he was 'exalted to the highest place'. That is the logic of verse 9. Having given up the glories of heaven for our sake (verse 6), Jesus has them restored. Those who knew their Old Testament well would instantly have heard echoes of Isaiah as the letter of Philippians was first read out. This is what he had said, centuries before:

> '... And there is no God apart from me,
> a righteous God and a Saviour;
>> there is none but me.
>
> 'Turn to me and be saved,
>> all you ends of the earth;
>> for *I am God, and there is no other* ...
> *Before me every knee will bow;*
>> *by me every tongue will swear.*
> They will say of me, "In the LORD alone
>> are righteousness and strength."'
> (Isaiah 45:21–24; my emphasis)

The Jesus who died on the cross is none other than the one true God, who revealed himself centuries ago through Isaiah, manifest in the flesh. The day will come when we shall all be forced to face facts and bow the knee before him. This will be the case whether or not we have done so during our lives. If you have not yet accepted his offer of mercy and forgiveness, then surely it is far better to come to him for life now while the offer still stands. There will be nothing worse than having to acknowledge as Lord the one who has no choice but to respond, 'I never knew you. Away from me, you evildoers!' (Matthew 7:23).

Studying the cross will have brought you face to face with the true character of God. It will have been uncomfortable, because whenever that happens, we are always forced to confront our own character and life with complete honesty; but it should also have been liberating, because you will have come to appreciate the wonderful love God has for all who come to him. Come to him, the one who is Lord of all, the one who died on the cross that you might have life; and once you have come to him, stick with him! Keep what he did at the cross central to your life. There he proved his love for you once and for all time.

The end of *Saving Private Ryan* is intensely moving. The captain, played by Tom Hanks, and most of his squad end up fatally wounded after trying to hold a bridge; but at least their mission has been accomplished: Private Ryan is safe. The big question is, was it worth it? It is impossible to answer. However, the dying words of Tom Hanks's character have to be some of the cruellest last words on film. Hardly able to speak, the dying captain whispers to Private Ryan his final command: 'Earn it! Earn it!' In other words, live such a life that gives the overwhelming loss of life purpose. 'Earn it!' They are cruel words, not least because it is clear that Ryan has been thinking like this anyway. To have it spoken aloud only makes the burden on him heavier. And it is a terrible burden. The film then closes with a scene in the present day as the now slightly doddery Ryan kneels at the captain's grave in a Normandy war cemetery. Tears stream down his cheek as he says to his wife, 'Tell me I've been good. Tell me I've lived a good enough life.'

Can you imagine if Jesus' dying words on that cross were, 'Earn it!' Can you imagine how much greater the burden would be? To earn the death of the one we worship as God! The pressure would be overwhelming. We could never do it. Instead, Jesus cried, 'It is finished.' The message of the cross is simply that we can never earn it; nor do we need to. How do we respond to that? Well, in one sense, we can't. It's too much. In another sense, there is only one way – to love our God with all our heart, mind, strength and soul. In other words, to worship our God. Not to earn God's love, but to revel in his love; not to persuade God to love us, but to delight in his love.

During the Middle Ages, a story circulated about Martin of Tours, a Christian after whom Martin Luther was named. It was said that Satan appeared to Martin in the guise of Jesus. Martin was ready to fall to his feet and worship this vision. Then suddenly, he looked up at the vision's feet and hands and asked, 'Where are the nail marks?' At that, the apparition vanished. The mark of true Christian living is that it has Jesus at the centre. This is not any Jesus, however; it is not to be a Jesus who is the figment of our imaginations. He must be the *crucified* Jesus. Our temptation will always be to sideline this. To quote one writer, the constant pressure will be to want 'a God without wrath who took [human beings] without sin into a kingdom without justice through the ministrations of a Christ without a cross'.[6] That pressure must be resisted at all costs, since this is the polar opposite of the Christian message. The *crucified* Christ will be the subject of the songs of heaven for eternity. We can join now in that glorious song, as we worship him with our lives and our lips. The only question that remains is, 'Will you too join in one day?'

And they sang a new song:

'You are worthy to take the scroll
    and to open its seals,
because you were slain,
    and with your blood you purchased men for God
    from every tribe and language and people and nation.

You have made them to be a kingdom and priests to serve our
     God,
   and they will reign on the earth.'

Then I looked and heard the voice of many angels, numbering
thousands upon thousands, and ten thousand times ten thousand.
They encircled the throne and the living creatures and the elders.
In a loud voice they sang:

'Worthy is the Lamb, who was slain,
to receive power and wealth and wisdom and strength
and honour and glory and praise!'

Then I heard every creature in heaven and on earth and under
the earth and on the sea, and all that is in them, singing:

'To him who sits on the throne and to the Lamb
be praise and honour and glory and power,
         for ever and ever!'

The four living creatures said, 'Amen', and the elders fell down and
worshipped.
(Revelation 5:9–14)

Study guide

This study guide is designed to be useful both to small groups and individuals. When used in groups, it is hoped that the leader will simply use the guide as a springboard to further discussion, tailor-made to suit the group's needs. Alternatively, since most chapters are based on one or two biblical passages, groups could be encouraged to read the relevant chapter of *Cross-Examined* prior to the group study and then be led through an inductive study on the relevant biblical passage(s).

Part 1. Cross-examined

1. In the dock (John 18)

1. How do your personal experiences and what you know of human history challenge belief in God's goodness, power and justice? Which of these do you find the hardest claim about God to accept (pp. 11–13)?

2. Spend some time working through one (or more, if you have time) of the accounts of Jesus' final days and identify

the ways in which he is shown to be in control of events (it will help to make notes as you go along). At each point, see if you can identify what the Gospel writer points to as Jesus' purpose behind the events (pp. 14ff.).

- Matthew 21:1–46; 26:1 – 27:66
- Mark 11:1 – 12:12; 14:1 – 15:47
- Luke 19:28 – 20:19; 22:1 – 23:56
- John 17:1 – 19:42

3. Pilate appears to have dismissed Jesus out of political expediency and fear of the mob (p. 17). Others in history have dismissed him for different reasons. For what reasons do you think that you, and those you know, are tempted to do the same?

2. 'You can't believe that, can you?' (1 Corinthians 1:18–25)

1. What factors make Jesus' claim to be sent from God appear so implausible (pp. 20–21)?

2. What parallels (if any) are there between Corinthian culture and your own (pp. 24–27)? What challenges do these present for explaining the Christian message to those around you?

3. '[Jesus] knew that such demands [e.g. for miracles] demonstrate a desire to dictate terms to God' (p. 27). How do you fall into the same trap? What is God's response (1 Corinthians 1:19–20)?

Part 2. Hard to accept, but hard to hide

3. United nations (Romans 3:9–20; Genesis 2:9 – 3:7)

1. 'But there is one thing of which I am absolutely certain: the reality of sin' (p. 33).

   '[Jesus] asserts in Mark 7 that sin is not primarily an external force or an environmental pressure, but is heart-driven' (p. 36). How would you go about defending these assertions?

2. What do you think was Paul's motivation in compiling his string of Old Testament verses about human sin (Romans 3:10–18)? Was he merely trying to assert his moral superiority (as so many assume is happening when Christians talk about sin), or did he have some other purpose (pp. 33ff.)?

3. Think back to a recent occasion when you gave in to a particular (or even regular) temptation. With Genesis 3 open in front of you, analyse any parallels between your own thought processes and the way that the man and woman were lured by the serpent into disobedience in Eden (p. 40). *(This is perhaps more for personal reflection than group discussion!)*

4. 'You can write the rules of your own life in religious language, or in the language of the street . . . it makes no difference' (p. 41). Why is there no difference before God between the respectably religious and the deliberately rebellious?

4. Fatal addiction (Genesis 3)

1. What is the connection between *feeling* guilty and *being* guilty (pp. 47–48)? What happens when you have either one without the other?

   'Just pick up today's newspaper. The alienating effect of sin is visible on every front page . . .' (p. 51). 'In a genuine sense, sin is an addiction' (p. 52).

   Are these claims valid and, if so, how? It might be worth actually opening a newspaper alongside one of the passages studied (e.g. Genesis 3, Romans 3 or Titus 3:3) to make your case.

2. Why is death the inevitable consequence of sin (p. 57)?

5. Divine justice (Isaiah 6; Romans 1:18 – 2:6)

1. What connotations does the word 'holiness' have in your mind? How aligned are they to the word's scriptural roots (pp. 60–61)?

2. Work through the passages alluded to on page 62 that refer to God's love in the Old Testament and his justice in the New Testament. How are these concepts compatible?

3. 'If we try to downplay either [God's justice or wrath], we end up in a far more frightening situation than if we hold on to them. For the truth is that we actually *need* God's justice and wrath' (pp. 61–62). How is this the case? Do you agree? Why? Reflect on your answers to this and compare them with your answers to question 1 (in Part 1).

4. What evidence is there in the world that God is a God of justice and therefore judges sin (pp. 67ff.)?

Part 3. Messiah: God's gift

6. Messiah: the promise (Isaiah 7, 9, 53)

1. The Victorian preacher J. C. Ryle asserted that Christianity without the cross of Christ is like a 'sky without a sun ... a compass without a needle' (p. 74). What do you think he meant? Is he correct and, if so, why?

2. What qualified Jesus to be 'the perfect mediator between God and us' (p. 79)?

3. The idea of Jesus taking our punishment in our place (i.e. penal substitution), which thus achieves propitiation (see pp. 82–85), is highly controversial in some circles. Why do you think that is? How would you respond to friends who object to this doctrine? What does the Bible have to say on the subject?

7. Messiah: the execution (Mark 15)

1. 'This means we must be careful in describing Jesus' agony' (p. 91). Think of any depictions of Jesus' death that you have come across (whether in books, old-master paintings or recent movies). What do they convey about his suffering and death? How effective are they, and what are their limitations? How do they measure up to the New Testament portrayals?

2. What is the significance of Mark's 'fast-edit' to the temple (pp. 93–94)? Study Hebrews 10:19–25 to see how the writer of Hebrews applies the imagery.

3. The centurion saw Jesus' death and declared, 'Surely this man was the Son of God' (Mark 15:39 – see p. 96). How was

the centurion able to draw this conclusion? In the light of
(and perhaps in contrast to) your answers to question 4 (in
Part 1), would you conclude the same? Why/why not?

8. Messiah: the blood (Various)

1. 'According to the New Testament, everything flows from
   [Jesus'] substitutionary death. Penal substitution is not, as
   some suggest, one illustrative model among many, from
   which we can choose what we like best. It is the *primary
   model* on which all the others depend' (pp. 100–101). Work
   through each of the four consequences of the cross outlined
   in this chapter and establish the validity of this assertion.

2. Why can't God 'just forgive'? Why did he have to go
   through the horror and complexities of the cross (pp. 105ff.)?

3. Why do you think that George Bernard Shaw was so
   offended by what he called 'crosstianity' (p. 115)?

9. Messiah: the triumph (Various)

1. In what sense is Jesus' resurrection a vindication of
   everything that he came to achieve (pp. 122ff.)?

2. What God achieves at the cross appears (initially at least)
   to be a direct challenge to the assertion of Proverbs 17:15
   (p. 132). How would you counter this charge?

3. Because of the cross, we can know 'that we cannot be loved
   any more than we are by God; nor can we be loved any
   less' (p. 120). How might you help those who struggle to
   know that God really does love them (pp. 131–132)? To
   which Bible passages might you point them, and how
   would you explain their relevance?

Part 4. Raised to life: so live it!

10. A life made possible (Various)

1. What are the causes of some people's mistaken belief that Christians want to pass on the gospel simply 'to make people feel bad' (p. 137)? How can we ensure that this doesn't happen?

2. Why is it necessary to keep repentance and faith together (pp. 138–142)?

3. It has been claimed that the vast majority of common pastoral problems can be sorted out by careful explanation of the so-called 'three tenses of resurrection' (as outlined on pp. 143–153). Why might this be the case?

11. A cross-shaped life (Mark 8; Philippians 2)

1. 'Jesus [was] no more than the mastermind behind a uniquely successful cult' (p. 155). How would you respond to this charge?

2. What did Spurgeon mean when he said, 'There are no crown-wearers in heaven who were not cross-bearers here below' (p. 159)? How do Mark 8 and Philippians 2 support his assertion?

3. What noticeable difference is made to your lifestyle and outlook by the fact that Jesus' final cry was, 'It is finished', and not, 'Earn it' (pp. 167–168)?

Notes

1. In the dock

1 *Telegraph Magazine*, 24 June 2000, p. 52.

2 Quoted in Gary A. Haugen, *Good News about Injustice* (IVP, 1999), p. 113.

3 C. S. Lewis, *God in the Dock* (Fount, 1979), p. 100.

4 See John 11:49–52.

5 D. A. Carson, *The Gospel according to John* (IVP, 1991), p. 583.

6 Carson, *John*, p. 584.

2. 'You can't believe that, can you?'

1 Quoted in *Third Way* 22.7 (September 1999), p. 25.

2 P. D. James, *The Children of Men* (Penguin, 1994), p. 73.

3 Crucifixion was regarded by first-century Judaism as a form of execution by hanging.

4 Quoted in *Third Way* 22.7 (September 1999).

5 For an introduction to what Paul was up against, see the article on 'Philosophy', in G. F. Hawthorne, R. P. Martin and D. G. Reid (eds.), *Dictionary of Paul and his Letters* (IVP, 1993), pp. 713–718.

3. United nations

1 A journalist in the *New York Times* even wrote this at Queen Victoria's Diamond Jubilee twenty years later: '[America is] a part, and a great part, of the Greater Britain which seems so plainly destined to dominate this planet.' Denis Judd, *Empire* (Fontana, 1997), p. 131.

2 Judd, *Empire*, p. 117.

3 From the Preamble to *The Charter of the United Nations*.

4 In these verses, Paul combines Psalms 14:1–3 and 53:1–3 with Ecclesiastes 7:20.

5 She was referring to John Wesley and George Whitefield among others.

6 Arnold Dallimore, *George Whitefield*, vol. 1 (Banner of Truth, 1970), p. 132.

7 Paul quotes Psalms 5:9; 140:3; 10:7; and closes the string with Isaiah 59:7–8.

8 J. I. Packer, *Concise Theology* (IVP, 1993), pp. 83–84.

9 Ravi Zacharias, *Deliver us from Evil* (Word, 1996), p. 148.

10 John Stott, *Evangelical Truth* (IVP, 1999), p. 88.

11 Gordon J. Wenham, *Genesis 1 – 15*, Word Biblical Commentary (Word, 1991), p. 90.

12 See, for example, God's prohibition on murder on account of people retaining his image (Genesis 9:6).

13 To follow this up in considerable depth, see Henri Blocher's masterly *Original Sin* (Apollos, 1997).

4. Fatal addiction

1 Fay Weldon, 'Inspector Remorse', *A Hard Time to be a Father* (Flamingo, 1998), p. 100.

2 S. E. Wirt and K. Beckstrom (eds.), *Living Quotations for Christians* (Hodder & Stoughton, 1974), p. 225.

3 Daniel Hans, in *U.S. News and World Report*, spring 1983.

4 Bernhard Schlink, *The Reader* (Phoenix, 1997), p. 196.

5 Erich Fromm, *The Sane Society* (Fawcett, 1977), p. 181.

6 Oscar Wilde, *An Ideal Husband*, Act 1.

7 Richard Baukham, 'First Steps to a Theology of Nature', *Evangelical Quarterly* 57 (1986), p. 240.

8 Figure taken from research by Dr Meg Barker, quoted in the *Daily Telegraph*, 23 September 2000.

9 Ravi Zacharias, *Can Man Live Without God?* (Word, 1994), p. 256.

10 For instance, Numbers 19:11–22 (dead bodies); Leviticus 11 (foods); Leviticus 13 – 14 (infectious disease).

11 Lord Bryon, from *Childe Harold's Pilgrimage*, Canto IV, lines 88–90.

12 Wenham, *Genesis 1 – 15*, p. 90.

13 H. Blocher, *In the Beginning* (IVP, 1984), p. 171.

14 For instance, Genesis 5:5, 8, 11, 14, 17, and so on.

15 Quoted in *The Meaning of Life*, a UCCF evangelistic resource.

5. Divine justice

1 Alec Motyer, *The Prophecy of Isaiah* (IVP, 1993), p. 77.

2 J. I. Packer, *Concise Theology* (IVP, 1993), p. 43.

3 Don Cormack, *Killing Fields, Living Fields* (Monarch, 1997), p. 450.

4 From an article by Elizabeth Becker, quoted in Cormack, *Killing Fields, p. 181*.

5 Bernard Levin, *The Times*, 22 April 1976.

6 Quoted in the *Daily Telegraph*, 12 April 2000. This is a cynical reference to Senator Edward Kennedy's 1969 car crash, which killed only one passenger.

7 Ravi Zacharias, *Deliver us from Evil* (Word, 1996), p. 178.

8 Peter Lewis, 'Walking Tall, Fallen Short', *Rescue!* (Christian Focus, 1995), p. 21.

9 Packer, *Theology*, p. 44.

10 Quoted in the *Daily Telegraph*, 4 May 1999.

11 See Dick Dowsett's *God, That's not Fair!* (OMF, 1982) or John Blanchard's *Whatever Happened to Hell?* (Evangelical Press, 1993).

6. Messiah: the promise

1 Quoted in John R. W. Stott, *Evangelical Truth* (IVP, 1999), p. 85.

2 Alec Motyer, *The Prophecy of Isaiah* (IVP, 1993), p. 83.

3 Motyer, *Isaiah*, p. 85. Motyer provides a succinct and helpful defence of this conclusion, including various other Old Testament instances of Isaiah's word.

4 For example, Exodus 20:7; Leviticus 24:13–16.

5 For example, read John 11:35; Luke 22:39–46; Hebrews 2:18; 4:15–16.

6 David Ewing Duncan, *The Calendar* (Fourth Estate, 1998), pp. 27–28.

7 C. E. B. Cranfield, *The Epistle to the Romans*, vol. 1 (T. & T. Clark, 1975), p. 217.

7. Messiah: the execution

1 *The Times*, 7 February 1952, p. 6.

2 Nicky Gumbel, *Questions of Life* (Kingsway, 1993), p. 35.

3 Louis de Bernières, *Captain Corelli's Mandolin* (Minerva, 1995), pp. 324–325.

4 Alec Motyer, *The Prophecy of Isaiah* (IVP, 1993), p. 78.

5 John R. W. Stott, *The Cross of Christ* (IVP, 1986), p. 159.

6 R. S. Thomas captured this self-sacrificial love in his wonderful, thought-provoking poem, 'The Coming'. R. S. Thomas, *Collected Poems*, 1945–1990 (Phoenix, 1995), p. 234.

8. Messiah: the blood

1 Leon Morris, *The Cross in the New Testament* (Paternoster, 1995), p. 219.

2 Handley Moule, *Charles Simeon* (IVF, 1965), pp. 25–26.

3 Abridged from A. Naismith, *1200 Notes, Quotes and Anecdotes* (Pickering & Inglis, 1963), p. 109.

4 C. S. Lewis, *Mere Christianity* (Fontana, 1955), p. 101.

5 Carnegie Simpson, quoted in John R. W. Stott, *The Cross of Christ* (IVP, 1986), p. 88.

6 Quoted in East *Asia's Billions* (OMF), April 2000, p. 10.

7 Quoted in *Word in Action* (Bible Society), March 2000, pp. 2–3.

8 *The Times*, 11 December 1997.

9 See, for instance, Shaw's introduction to his play *Major Barbara*, which can be found at the following website: <www.best.com/~hansen/DrPseudocryptonym/Shaw_MajorBarbara.html>.

10 David Gooding, *True to the Faith* (Hodder & Stoughton, 1990), p. 220.

11 Abridged from a story in Robert E. Coleman, *Written in Blood* (Revell, 1972), p. 32.

9. Messiah: the triumph

1 Quoted by Clifton Fadiman (ed.), *The Faber Book of Anecdotes* (Faber & Faber, 1985), p. 495.

2 Fadiman, *Anecdotes*, p. 468.

3 N. T. Wright, *Colossians and Philemon*, Tyndale New Testament Commentary (IVP, 1986), p. 116 (his italics).

4 See article on 'Satan', *New Bible Dictionary*, 2nd ed. (IVP, 1982).

5 Read, for instance, Frank Morison's Who *Moved the Stone?* (Faber & Faber, 1944) and Sir Norman Anderson's *The Evidence for the Resurrection* (IVP, 1950).

6 Ravi Zacharias, *Can Man Live without God?* (Word, 1994), p. 295.

7 Pinchas Lapide, *The Resurrection of Jesus: A Jewish Perspective* (SPCK, 1984), pp. 69, 126, 92.

8 Clayborne Carson (ed.), *The Autobiography of Martin Luther King, Jr* (Little, Brown, 1999), p. 232.

9 P. T. Forsyth, quoted in John R. W. Stott, *The Cross of Christ* (IVP, 1986), p. 336.

10 Bernhard Schlink, *The Reader* (Phoenix, 1997), p. 156.

11 D. A. Carson, *How Long, O Lord?* (IVP, 1990), p. 183.

10. A life made possible

1 Douglas Coupland, *Girlfriend in a Coma* (Flamingo, 1998), p. 81.

2 Coupland, *Girlfriend*, pp. 81–82.

3 Coupland, *Girlfriend*, p. 83.

4 Elbert Hubbard, *Leadership* 15.4 (October 1994).

5 *Concise Oxford Dictionary of Current English* (OUP, 1990).

6 See Romans 8:9; Acts 16:7; Galatians 4:6.

7 *Fantasy Rooms*, BBC2, 5 July 2000.

11. A cross-shaped life

1 Quoted in John R. W. Stott, *The Cross of Christ* (IVP, 1986), p. 282.

2 Erwin W. Lutzer, *Hitler's Cross* (Moody, 1995), pp. 181–182.

3 Elisabeth Elliot, *Shadow of the Almighty* (OM, 1988), p. 15.

4 Quoted (with original italics) from the Heaven's Gate website: <http://heavensgatetoo.com>.

5 Primo Levi, *If This Is a Man* (Abacus, 1987), p. 127.

6 Attributed to the theologian Reinhold Niebuhr.

Suggestions for further reading

If you read only one other book:
John R. W. Stott, *The Cross of Christ* (IVP, 1986).

Also helpful:
D. A. Carson, *The Cross and Christian Ministry* (IVP, 1993)
Leon Morris, *The Atonement* (IVP, 1983)
Leon Morris, *The Cross of Jesus*, Biblical and Theological Classics
    Library (Paternoster, 1994)
Vaughan Roberts, *Turning Points* (OM, 1999)
Derek Tidball, *The Message of the Cross*, The Bible Speaks Today
    (IVP, 2001)

For reference:
Bruce Milne, *Know the Truth*, 2nd ed. (IVP, 1998)
J. I. Packer, *Concise Theology* (IVP, 1993)

Scripture index

The entries in bold refer to the specific passages cited at the beginning of the chapters.

SCRIPTURE INDEX | 189